Tomorrow's Super Teacher

Tomorrow's Super Teacher

Changing Teacher Education to
Nurture Culturally Sustaining Educators

Chateé Omísadé Richardson

ROWMAN & LITTLEFIELD
Lanham • Boulder • New York • London

Published by Rowman & Littlefield
A wholly owned subsidiary of The Rowman & Littlefield Publishing Group, Inc.
4501 Forbes Boulevard, Suite 200, Lanham, Maryland 20706
www.rowman.com

6 Tinworth Street, London SE11 5AL, United Kingdom

British Library Cataloguing in Publication Information Available

Library of Congress Cataloging-in-Publication Data

Names: Richardson, Chateé Omísadé, 1979- author.
Title: Tomorrow's super teacher : changing teacher preparation to nurture
  culturally sustaining educators / Chateé Omísadé Richardson.
Description: Lanham : Rowman & Littlefield, [2020] | Includes
  bibliographical references. | Summary: "This book discusses the history
  of the education system leading up to current challenges in order to
  present a picture of how we have arrived at the current state of k-12
  education in the United States"—Provided by publisher.
Identifiers: LCCN 2020018620 (print) | LCCN 2020018621 (ebook) | ISBN
  9781475856170 (cloth) | ISBN 9781475856187 (paperback) | ISBN
  9781475856194 (epub)
Subjects: LCSH: Education—United States—History. | Education—Aims and
  objectives—United States. | Teachers—Training of—United States.
Classification: LCC LA11 .R42 2020 (print) | LCC LA11 (ebook) | DDC
  370.973—dc23
LC record available at https://lccn.loc.gov/2020018620
LC ebook record available at https://lccn.loc.gov/2020018621

This book is dedicated to

my parents, Gary Richardson, Connie Richardson, and Nila Richardson, who raised me to be one of the ones who will change the world;

my daughters, Nyabinghi and Kioni, who are my heartbeats, my inspiration, and my everyday teachers;

my sister, Desirae, who taught me the essence of standing up for others and raising them up higher than yourself;

my guides, Barbara Gilmore, Lori Grace, and Robert Browning, thank you for showing me the essence of love when I most needed it and saving my life;

my mirrors, Tawede, Nzingha, Dzifa, Osuntoki, Okiki Ola, Ananse Kounda;

all of the elders and teachers who have touched my life (the good and the bad as discomfort can facilitate growth);

my students, who inspire me every day to be my absolute best;

and all those superhero teachers who do this noble and important work every single day of the school year.

I see you!

Contents

~

Preface

Simply put . . .
Education brings knowledge . . .
Knowledge is said to be power . . .
Knowledge is also responsibility . . .
So there is responsibility in education . . .
You are responsible for *what* you teach . . .
You are responsible for *how* you educate . . .
Education should not be imbalanced . . .
Education should not be alienating . . .
Education should not be damaging . . .
Education should not be subjugating . . .
Subjugation limits opportunity . . .
Education should provide opportunity . . .
Education should not take it away . . .
Education should initiate growth . . .
Growth that may be momentarily uncomfortable . . .
But brings comfort after you have been stretched . . .
Stretching allows and inspires creativity . . .
Creativity circles back to power . . .
Power that reflects freedom . . .
Education should be freedom!

What kind of educator will you choose to be?
What will *you* allow?

Will you continue with the regular . . . contribute to business as usual?
This book provides information to inspire *your* choice.
Do not choose to be regular . . .
Choose to be extraordinary.
There are no lines . . . color where you will . . .

~

Introduction

We teach what we value.

—Gloria Ladson-Billings

During the 180 instructional days that youth are in school each year, they spend significantly more waking hours at school with teachers than they do at home with their own parents. This alone hints at the substantial impact teachers have on student thoughts, beliefs, attributions, and actions. An educator friend recently shared with me that she called a student's parents about a behavior issue and the parent responded by saying, "She's with you more than she is with me so isn't this really *your* concern? I don't call *you* when she acts up on the weekends."

She was dead serious! Though this response is hilarious in many ways, it floored me for others. It made me think past my knee jerk, "get your child together" reaction and deeper into the role teachers play in student outcomes, both short and long term.

It made me think about how teachers literally shape the future both by what they teach and by *how* they teach. The content and the quality are both salient. In my student interactions over the past fifteen years kindergarten through college, I have come to understand that students tend to remember two types of teachers, those who were warm and connected with them in some way positively, and those who leave a negative impression through words (which carry their own special power) or deeds.

I would like to ask you to take a moment, sit back, close your eyes, and think about all of the educators you have encountered. Whom do you remember? Why do you remember them? Was it something they did? Something they said? How did they make you feel (big or small)?

Engaging in this activity myself, I vividly remember two such teachers who live at opposite ends of the spectrum in my memory. There are many who exist in between that I can recall here and there, like Ms. Frazier who was everyone's favorite because she always had a good story to tell beginning with "Shut the windows and close the doors people, I have something to say!" These two, however, stand out because I vividly remember how being in their classes made me feel.

They left an enduring impact. I understand how their styles and messages shaped me in different ways, leading to the type of educator I have become and the charge I have taken up to change the system, to affect the world. For the sake of transparency, and to make my point, I will be candid in my descriptions, but I will call the teacher who left negative residue on my impressionable mind Ms. M to keep her identity confidential. I would like to extend her the courtesy of protecting her, even though protecting me was never her priority.

The Curious Case of Ms. M

Ms. M had a reputation at my school for being both mean and unforgiving. The tea passed through the halls down through all the classes was that she did not like Black people and she did not like men. It was simply apparent to us in her dealings with students and the way she discussed content.

She was very brusque and generally impatient. We generally dreaded going to her class. She had a file full of complaints and a reputation for downplaying them by turning attention to the student involved. She did not pause to ensure our understanding of material. She kept going, and if you got it, then you got it. If you did not, well, then you did not. And it was you who were not up to par. She taught AP/IB English.

When I took her class, there were three Black people in it, including myself. The three of us banded together to support one another. Two of us vowed to get the highest grades in the class when she communicated to us that she questioned the intellect of people who looked like us. It was difficult for me to understand why she did not like me. Literally *all* of the teachers liked me. I was given the Teacher's Pet award due to (my classmates hating on) the amount of love my teachers had for me. I suspected that her reputation had something to do with it. Then little things she would say in class confirmed it for me.

I distinctly recall her using the N word quite comfortably when we read *The Heart of Darkness*. In fact, she used a parallel term that was not found in the book, catching everyone off guard. She also told the class that the only reason Toni Morrison received the Nobel Prize for Literature was because they needed a "token Black person."

I wondered then, and I wonder now, who could read Toni Morrison's words and say something like that? Ms. M, that is who! I could continue, but I think you get the point of the type of messages she transmitted to us. Not only were these things hurtful to us, they also shaped the way our classmates viewed us specifically, Black people in general, and the quality and capacity of Black intellect.

At the culmination of the course, my friend and I were discussing our grades (as we worked our tails off to receive the highest scores). We were also discussing the colleges we were accepted to and the fact that we were selected as International Ambassadors for homecoming (this was what my school did rather than having a king and a queen). Ms. M approached us and sarcastically said, "Congratulations. I didn't think you could do it, but you did."

That was the first and last time congratulations felt like a physical slap to the face. Ms. M made me feel unwelcomed, invisible, incapable, and miscellaneous—feelings that I will *never* forget and that I *never* want to engender within anyone else. I will say that pushing myself to exceed her low expectations made me a solid writer, but not all students carry the same level of resilience.

The Canorous Case of Mr. Halvorson

Mr. Scott Halvorson on the other hand made me feel welcomed, confident, seen, and valued. He met us at the door every single day of the school year with smiles, handshakes, and high fives. He knew every single name of every student and how to pronounce it correctly (this is so important), no matter how foreign it might feel to the tongue. He also added his own witty and endearing nickname for each of us.

I was Chateé Chateau Chapeau, which he pronounced with his best rendition of a French accent. He took the time to learn the story of my name and apply it, establishing a different type of connection. My friend Susan was Susan Thrash Metal Thrasher. There was also Lisa Precise Sais.

The first day of class, he explained to us that he wanted us to be "loud, strong, and wrong," a concept I have continued using with students in my charge. He said that we were all brilliant and he wanted to hear our voices because we all had something to say, that we should not fear saying the wrong thing because we were *all* learning. If we said the wrong thing, so what? Who cares! At least we had the courage to speak out. If you answered and it was not the response he was looking for, he would enthusiastically say, "No, that is not it, however, I *love* your enthusiasm." We would be left smiling, ready to respond again.

I could probably stop gushing about Mr. Halvorson where I tell you that because of him I absolutely loved reading Homer's *The Iliad* and *The Odyssey*. He allowed us to take the lead on deciphering text and translating the old English–style speech into understandable and time-applicable terms for our peers. He sealed the deal at the end of the lesson when he allowed us to litigate a court case deciding who was responsible for starting the Trojan War. Out of everyone, I was given the role of Helen of Troy. I never felt so beautiful, seen, and empowered in one of my classes.

Other students played Aphrodite, Hera, Paris, Agamemnon, Menelaus, Hector, and so on and so on. Each of us was given the charge to build a case proving our innocence and pinning the responsibility for the war on someone else, utilizing evidence from the text to support our claims. Students were also assigned to be the judge and members of the jury so that everyone had a role and the decisions were in the hands of the students.

I won the case! I implicated Aphrodite because it was she who used her powers to make Helen fall in love with Paris to reward him for choosing her as the most beautiful goddess. Twenty-five years later, I remember adding evidence that the actions of the other characters were all reactionary to this moment. He taught me how to create a sound argument and to solidly support my point. I remember how much fun we all had completing this assignment and settling the case in class.

He also mildly taught us advocacy and the immense power of prose. He wrote an eloquent response to a newspaper article criticizing the movie *Forest Gump* (1994) called "Time to Dump the Gump." The author criticized the movie for trivializing important issues, sending the message that success has nothing to do with intelligence and hard work, and for being both anachronistic and elitist.

Mr. Halvorson penned a response to the editor praising the movie for its brilliance. His response reached the director of the film, Robert Zemeckis, who contacted Mr. Halvorson directly. He arranged for his students to have lunch (at our so-called inner-city school no less) with Robert Zemeckis and

Mykelti Williamson, who played Bubba Blue in the film. We were included in his moment. We felt important.

The Message

As I have studied development and come to understand how people learn, I realized that Mr. Halvorson was engaging in culturally sustaining practice. Could it have been training that made him particularly culturally astute? I am not sure. I do not know if he was even trying to be culturally responsive. However, I do know that he was an anomaly in my experience.

Literally one teacher in fifty-nine over twelve years of schooling. I honestly believe that this was just what was in him to do. He is an exemplar of an actual living breathing advocate for his students. I recently found an email I sent him in May 2012:

> It's me . . . Chateé (Chateau, Chapeau) . . . do you even remember me. You taught me for 9th and 10th grade English. I had to find you to say hello, see how you are, and to tell you how much you have inspired me. You were the BEST English teacher I have EVER had, and my favorite teacher from High School. I now have a BA in Drama, an MA in Counseling Psychology and I am finishing my PhD at Georgia State University in Educational Psychology. This is part of your legacy. I would love to see where all of your students are today! I teach a course for pre-service teachers at GSU (which forces them to explore and confront their personal biases in terms of race, class, gender, sexual orientation, spirituality, etc.) and I use you and your methods as examples of exemplary teaching = 0). Because of you I STILL love The Iliad and The Odyssey AND I have no fear of putting myself out there to answer questions. I tell everyone that Scott Halvorson taught me to be "loud, strong, and wrong!!!" I am teaching my four year old daughter to do the same thing = 0). I just wanted to say thank you for the role you played in establishing my love of literature and words! I have a vivid memory of playing Helen of Troy in the class trial of who was responsible for the Trojan War, as well as the letter you wrote in the newspaper responding to the article, Time to "Dump the Gump." I truly hope all is well with you.

He responded saying "of course" he remembered me and telling me how proud he was of all that I had accomplished. He was humbled that I remembered so much, that I was so affected. We decided to remain in touch. These are the types of relationships and connections we should forge with students. A teacher should leave this kind of imprint on students—one that engenders confidence, reinforces self-efficacy, and leaves students understanding that there are no limits to the possibilities.

The reality is that there were probably also some good things that Ms. M did in the classroom. I am sure it was not *all* bad. The problem is that it was the bad that stuck. I cannot remember the good if it took place. The negative comments and experiences overshadow anything else.

The Call and the Purpose

Imagine if I had fifty-nine Mr. Halvorsons during my kindergarten through twelfth-grade experiences rather than just one. I ache for the children who have none. Now imagine how different my experience and her own outlook would have been if Ms. M had been guided and supported through confronting and challenging her biases in a meaningful way before she was allowed to teach. Not all students are resilient enough to fight against teachers who make disparaging and in many cases harmful remarks.

I have worked professionally with enough teachers over the past fifteen years to understand that some teachers know what they are doing and some unwittingly transmit these messages. They are not necessarily aiming to continue promoting patriarchy and monoculturalism. It is the curriculum that is the overarching problem—the curriculum taught in teacher education programs and the curriculum they are asked to teach once they are granted their own classrooms.

Teachers feel bound by it and the system. They need to be taught to confront limiting beliefs and given more freedom to create in ways that honor all experiences. This goes back to how we "prepare" our future educators. This is a deeply entrenched systemic issue.

With this book, *I am calling out* the American education system. *I am calling out* teacher education and preparation. It is way past time for us to change the script and prepare our teachers differently so that we can create a new kind of teacher leader—one who abhors the banking method of education (that creates automatons) and pours into all of their students in ways that ignite their passion for and commitment to lifelong learning and growth.

This work comes to you from the heart and experience of a passionate educator who was raised in California's Long Beach Unified School District and who has worked in schools with teachers and students in California, Nebraska, and in multiple school districts in Georgia. I have taught students in public, private, and independent school settings and observed in charter school contexts. I have worked for years to prepare teachers. I have seen pockets of awesomeness to rival the horror stories, where children fit into the space and find a rhythm that works with their own particular drumbeat.

What I have not witnessed (except in one instance, shout-out to Black Star Educational Institute, but this is another book for another time) in any public or private space is a holistic approach to education where the space fits the children, playing multiple cadences to blend with each student where they are. This will happen when we change the game. It is way past time to remix and change the game! If you are with me—if you are brave enough to face the facts—if you are ready to incite *real* change—please place your game token on the starting space on the game board by turning the page to chapter 1.

CHAPTER ONE

~

What Is Really Going On?

There are three principles on which human life flourishes [diversity, curiosity, and creativity] and they are contradicted by the culture of education under which most teachers have to labor and most students have to endure.

—Sir Ken Robinson

Introduction

This quote eloquently synthesizes the essence of the issue into a concise sentence. The current educational structure has, through time and inattention, been molded into a deep culture of monoculturalism, apathy, and stagnation. Each one of those terms (diversity, curiosity, and creativity) is lacking on a large scale within the current structure. It strikes a deep chord because education should be freeing, not endured.

To endure is to suffer through something that is particularly painful or difficult. The word *labor* here connotes toiling with difficulty. Education should be traversed, explored, and delighted in. It should spark a flame of excitement.

What happens to a light systematically dimmed by years of enduring? This question should be considered for both teachers and students. In order to explain how the system has arrived at this current state, which interestingly simultaneously happens to be the historical state in modern face, we must begin with the irony of the situation.

The State of Education

Recent research indicates that each year the population of the United States becomes increasingly more diverse (Hughes, 2003; Villegas & Lucas, 2007; Xu & Drame, 2008; Zhao, Meyers, & Meyers, 2009). This is due to the increasing number of immigrants and refugees entering U.S. borders, as well as to the increasing birthrate of diverse groups already living in the United States (Colby & Ortman, 2015; Villegas & Lucas, 2007). Overall, fertility rates are expected to decline across cultures in the coming years, and White students are expected to become the minority numerically.

Amos (2016) reports that students of color will be approximately 50 percent of the population by 2020. According to Colby and Ortman (2015), population projections from 2014 to the year 2060 indicate that by 2044 more than half of all Americans will be members of a group that is currently considered to be minority, and by 2060 one in five Americans will be foreign-born citizens. Because of the influx of diverse Americans, students from linguistically diverse backgrounds have been identified as the fastest growing K–12 population.

It is problematic that although this population is growing steadily and will at some point collectively surpass the number of White students enrolled in U.S. schools, they continue to be marginalized and ignored in the educational system (Renner et al., 2004). Amos (2016) also states that the majority of teachers will likely continue to be predominantly White. *The State of Racial Diversity in the Educator Workforce* report published in 2016 reported that 82 percent of public school teachers were White, education leaders (administrators) were also predominantly White, and this number is not expected to shift much, even as the student population culturally transmutes.

Teachers are also expected to continue to be majority women, middle class, and Christian. This is a profound argument for the inclusion of a greater focus on culture and pluralism in all preservice teacher programs. This mismatch holds academic, emotional, and social consequences for students who experience marginalization (CAEP, 2015).

According to Thompson (2015a), a culturally pluralistic society is one in which a number of minority cultures exist within the context of a larger dominant culture. A feature of pluralism is value and respect for minority cultures by the groups themselves and the majority culture. As the United States has theoretically been thought to both represent and embrace cultural pluralism in a general sense, this perceived acceptance has not spread into the systemic frame of the country in terms of laws, policies, and educational infrastructure, all of which still retain features of institutionalized racism.

The education system in America is based on the mainstream/majority culture. This means that it reflects Anglo-Puritan beliefs, creating a space of marginalization for youth who do not ascribe to this particular ideology. Preservice teacher candidates are consistently taught and trained only within this frame.

The Encyclopedia of Diversity and Social Justice defines marginalization as "the experience of social disadvantage or exclusion of individuals or groups that find people perceiving that they or others are on the fringes of society" (Thompson, 2015b, p. 495). The definition goes on to explain that this social exclusion from economic, mainstream cultural, and/or political life is deeply entrenched along scientifically and socially constructed racial lines. It manifests as unbalanced power dynamics that play out in schools and society.

This creates an opportunity gap for people who fall within the margins and can have a negative impact on not only them but also their descendants. People pass their socialization down, leaving a significant impact on future generations. Other marginalized groups can include elderly citizens, those with mental or physical disabilities, and single mothers

Further identifying marginalization as a face of oppression, Young (2004) adds that it is in many ways worse than exploitation. In this case society has either not considered the group in question or made the decision that they are not worth including in any way, which contributes to a sense of powerlessness for members of that group. It has long been understood that race and categorical difference craft the context for power and social dominion in America.

An extension of this is the fact that one perspective is protected and held higher in esteem than all others to the exclusion and sometimes defamation of everything else (Grant & Gillespie, 1993; Ladson-Billings, 2017; Paris, 2012). Because the aspect of society that is protected is the majority White culture, Young (2004) states that marginalization is very closely linked to Whiteness. Wise (2008) explains that Whiteness within the context of society describes beliefs, presuppositions, and attitudes stemming from the dominant cultural perspective. All one has to do is read curricular materials to see how this manifests in schooling.

This idea of marginalization is mirrored in the educational system. It is a microcosm that both reflects the ills of society and also populates the larger society feeding those ills, as youth graduate and join the workforce (Gregorčič, 2009; Singh, 2011). Just as people of color become confined to the outskirts through societal hegemony, so too do students of color become marginalized through scholastic hegemony as again the teaching force is overwhelmingly White and traditionally taught/trained from the same perspective. Until change is enacted, the cycle will only continue and it will worsen.

For the purposes of this book, marginalized students of color refers to members of the African American, Asian American, Indigenous American, and Latinx American communities as well as English language learners who experience intersectionality, or overlapping identities, within any of the aforementioned groups. It is important to note that the intersection of poverty also reinforces feelings of alienation specifically as it pertains to access to resources and power in social and educational spaces. However, the historical experience of poverty also connects back to racial construction and has sociopolitical implications (Thompson, 2015b).

Recent research and national testing results have revealed consistent gaps for students of color. African, Latinx, South Asian, and Indigenous American descent students continue to have lower test scores within the educational system when compared to their European American counterparts (National Assessment of Educational Progress, 2019). Academic failure, underachievement, disidentification, cultural mistrust, and stereotype threat have been widely discussed in relation to the educational experience of these students (Bailey & Paisley, 2004; Chavous et al., 2003; Ladson-Billings, 2014; Osborne, 1997; Steele, 1997).

The impetus for the disconnect has been identified as conflicting cultures (that is, mainstream American versus African/African American, Asian, Latino, or Indigenous) and the dismissal of alternate cultural realities from the American educational system (Bass & Coleman, 1997; Berry, 2003; Parsons, 2003). The conflict and disconnect exists within the curriculum as well as interactions with teachers. Teachers who are also socialized to believe these cultures have not made significant contributions.

Many researchers, psychologists, and educators have offered different theories in an attempt to explain the disparity between the educational achievement of culturally diverse students and White students. However, researchers, policy makers, and educators continue to struggle to identify and implement consistent and direct solutions to the problem (Dittmann, 2004; Chamberlin, 2005; Paris & Alim, 2014). In order to address the low academic achievement of marginalized students effectively, educators must find ways to draw them into the academic process in a way that is culturally relevant.

Using students' culture in the classroom has been found to be an effective way to incorporate them into the academic process, as cultural group membership has been found to be tied to specific ways of learning, thinking, and doing (Ladson-Billings, 1995b; Hilliard, 1997; Smith & Ayers, 2006). Students need to feel nurtured and safe in their academic environment, not intimidated by it. Culture and identity intersect in the academic setting in ways that allow one to either relate or disassociate within that domain.

Hammond (2015) discusses how a person's brain will not connect with others if they are perceived to be socially or psychologically threatening. It will literally disassociate. Therefore culturally sustaining curricula and pedagogy are essential tools that have positive implications for *all* classrooms, *all* academic arenas, and *all* students, not simply students of color.

Marginalization within educational spaces again mirrors the parent culture and engenders negative academic outcomes and a cloak of invisibility for affected learners. It can be argued then that just as American society holds the dominant culture in high esteem and perpetuates this perspective as an indicator of normalcy, so too does the American educational system (Henfield & Washington, 2012; Paris, 2012; Smith & Ayers, 2006; Wise, 2008). Anything that falls outside of this sphere is deemed less than or deficient.

Thus this system is also closely linked to the ideas of Whiteness and powerlessness. This ideology is supported and nourished as it transmits back into the parent culture when students leave school and merge with society through the workforce. By this time they have fermented a reality of cultural alienation and invisibility that is natural to the fabric of functioning in this country.

Singh (2011) states that children differ more when they exit the school system than they did when they entered it. School socializes children in certain ways. The parent society may highlight these differences in order to construct and validate cultural inequities and inequalities inherent in laws and policies.

Yes, it can absolutely be argued that some of these differences can simply be due to time and natural growth patterns. However, it is important to pay attention to fissures and separations caused specifically by the school experience itself. Feelings of alienation, invisibility, and voicelessness are directly attributed to the exclusion of culture and lived experience of diverse students as valid from the curriculum (Ali, Rohindra, & Coll, 2008; Boekaerts, 1998; Ladson-Billings, 1995a).

The Encyclopedia of Diversity and Social Justice goes on to explain that the lack of consideration of cultural ways of being merges with the application of negative labels, applied by administrators and teachers, which increases isolation in the educational system (Sefa Dei, 2008; Thompson, 2015b; Villegas & Lucas, 2007). Think back to the Curious Case of Ms. M shared in the introduction. Her words and actions merged with the curriculum, alienating her students and transmitting harmful messages.

Similarly, labels such as *token, disadvantaged, underachieving, oppressed, other, excluded, high risk, at-risk,* and many more lead to feelings of inferiority and inaccessibility. These experiences and labels affect youth in the classroom and follow them outside to their daily lives, leading to a lack of opportunity and social mobility. Overall lifelong functioning can be impaired and again can trickle down to affect future generations who inherit this from parents.

If education is to be truly effective with children from different cultural backgrounds, their learning histories should not only be acknowledged but should also be employed as the very foundation and vehicle for future learning. Cultural content must be integrated into the curriculum. The very way that individuals think, encode, and process information is predicated in cultural transmissions (Hammond, 2015; Ladson-Billings, 2017; Smith & Ayers, 2006; Stanley & Noblit, 2009).

Ignoring this is akin to ignoring the way the mind functions when attempting to teach. In acknowledgment of this, the question for each child should then become: What in the learning experience is meaningful and relevant for you based on your cultural reality? Teachers must begin to confront this question during preservice preparation within their core course load. This will create the understanding that this is a part of what it means to teach an individual, thus allowing them to make different connections with students from all backgrounds.

Preparing teachers to meet the needs of our diverse student population begins with preservice education. Teachers should become equipped to meet the needs of diverse learners while completing their teacher education program leading toward certification. Just as they are equipped with content knowledge and learning theory, teachers should learn that culture impacts these domains.

Unfortunately, there is consensus in the literature over the past twenty-four years that teacher preparation is lacking as it pertains to training future educators to acknowledge culture and to engage in sustaining practices (Castagno & Brayboy, 2008; Hsaio, 2015; Ellerbrock et al., 2016; Ladson-Billings, 2000, 2014; Renner et al., 2004; Siwatu, 2007; Thompson, 2015a; Villegas & Lucas, 2007; Zhao, Meyers, & Meyers, 2009). Diverse cultures have been treated as supplemental to the mandatory curriculum that highlights White theorists. When diversity is discussed, it is superficially glossed over.

This leads to educators who do not adequately integrate culture and who do not feel comfortable employing culturally responsive pedagogy (Hsaio,

2015; Ladson-Billings, 2014; Renner et al., 2004; Villegas & Lucas, 2007). The simple acquisition of knowledge, skills, and competence does not predict future behavior. Discussion does not necessarily translate into implementation (Pajares, 1996).

Culturally responsive teacher preparation has been identified as a method of mitigating the marginalization of students of color in the education system. It enhances student buy-in and the academic achievement of all children, not just those from culturally diverse backgrounds (Irving & Hudley, 2008; Hsaio, 2015; Kalyanpur & Harry, 1997; Kea & Utley, 1998; Ladson-Billings, 2000, 2006; Renner et al., 2004; Singh, 2011; Villegas & Lucas, 2002; Zhao, Meyers, & Meyers, 2009). In order to work toward achieving this lofty goal, a prime starting point is to examine what already exists out there in teacher education programs. Chapter 5 leads the reader through an examination of current programmatic offerings leading to the preparation of culturally aware educators who engage in culturally sustaining practice, educators who understand that this is simply what it means to teach.

Hollins (1993), Gay (2002), and Siwatu (2006) identified competencies for teaching diverse populations. Hsiao (2015) synthesized their work to create a working definition of culturally responsive teachers. It is further developed here to cultivate a prototype of culturally sustaining super teachers.

Super teachers are those who first challenge their own biases. They then identify students' needs and deliver culturally sustaining instruction, consistently enriching students' diverse overlapping and intersectional cultures. They also communicate with students and parents and design and implement curricula creating a caring and supporting educational setting.

Even after this explanation, some of you still might be wondering what culture has to do with it. You might be thinking that this does not pertain to you if you have a class full of White children. If we all exist under this American umbrella, why do we need to think about individual culture? We are a melting pot, right? Shouldn't we just be one people?

The next chapter centers on why cultural context is vital to changing the education game from something to be suffered through to something that creates space and opportunity for everyone. Even a class of all White students holds significant diversity. Turn the page to roll the die, move your game token forward, and collect game keys leading toward curricular freedom.

CHAPTER TWO

~

Three Steps Forward, Four Steps Back

An Overview of Education in America

I've noticed a fascinating phenomenon in my thirty years of teaching: schools and schooling are increasingly irrelevant to the great enterprises of the planet. No one believes anymore that scientists are trained in science classes or politicians in civics classes or poets in English classes. The truth is that schools don't really teach anything except how to obey orders.

—John Taylor Gatto, *Dumbing Us Down: The Hidden Curriculum of Compulsory Education*

Introduction

The school system worked exactly for whom and for what it was created at the time it was created. Things have changed greatly since then in terms of American culture in general and the workforce that the system is feeding. The great problem (and fascinating phenomenon) that this country has been facing for a while is that the school system did not change with the times.

This chapter presents a synopsis of the history of education in the United States, centering on its original purpose and focus and leading into the challenges in the current educational landscape. A detailed snapshot of arguably the most impacted community is provided to highlight the adverse effects this stagnant structure has had on generations of students. The goal is to present a complete picture of why changing the game now is vital to building an optimal future.

Figure 2.1. 1915 versus 2015. Credit: 1915, www.clevelandfoundation100.org (via Google Images); 2015, www.wskg.org (via Google Images).

The U.S. Educational System

According to Owens (2011) and Bennett (2015), the original purpose of education in America, from its inception, was to promote the retention of Judeo-Christian religious principles and practices—in other words, to perpetuate and sustain Christianity. This was coupled with the foundation of Anglo-Saxon culture transported from Britain and perpetuated through enslavement and indentured servitude systems. The focus of education took a shift in the 1700s to foster a productive society but held on to the Anglo-Christian underpinnings and still did not include those who were enslaved, as there were laws created forbidding them to learn.

In 1749, Benjamin Franklin penned a paper titled *Proposals to the Education of Youth*. This marked the beginning of an educational system focused on livelihood and occupation specifically for White youth. Through this proposed program of study, students would be taught to be obedient to authority, to think and act in a manner prescribed to be appropriate, and prepared to feed the industrial-based workforce of the time (Boykin, 2000; Owens, 2011; Young, 2004).

Thomas Jefferson later participated in solidifying the structure of American public schools by calling for funding for "grammar schools" during the late eighteenth century. Again, this system was created solely for the development of White children. He stated the purpose of the schools to be for the identification of "geniuses" who would be "raked from the rubbish" (Boykin, 2000). Thus, the proposed educational process would weed out subpar students and find the best and brightest who would lead the nation. The rest would again fall into place (in the margins) by learning obedience and feeding the workforce.

This structure perpetuates and encapsulates the idea of powerlessness, as it excluded youth of differing backgrounds, and for the White children it supported, those without the power (the so-called rubbish or subpar pupils) were ruled by those "identified" geniuses (Young, 2004). This begs the question of what characteristics were believed to constitute genius. This structure has remained the underlying foundation of American education since that time, and 270 years later, it unfortunately reflects recent educational statistics (National Assessment of Educational Progress, 2019).

According to Boykin (2000), the traditional or original American system operated on three prescribed functions and three assumptions that are still very prevalent in the structure of the current system (table 2.1).

Table 2.1. Structure of American Schools

Traditional Operating *Functions* of American Public Schools:
1. Sort and select students; weed out the best and the brightest to lead the nation.
2. Acculturate immigrants to mainstream American values and behaviors.
3. Socialize a workforce for factory-based occupation.

Traditional Operating *Assumptions* of American Public Schools:
1. Learners are passive.
2. Knowledge is accumulated by drill, repetition, and rote memorization.
3. Schools should be run as bureaucracies (hierarchically divided by categories).

Boykin (2000) asserts that the behaviorist ideologies of John Watson, the stimulus-response theory of Edward Thorndike, and the functionalist views of William James both shaped and drove practices of pedagogy during this time period, meaning the main focus was on changing and controlling behavior to function within prescribed boundaries. As there has not been much change, this is the same system that students of color were integrated into during desegregation in 1954, and it is the same system students of color are struggling through today.

This process did not then and does not now allow for critical or complex thinking allowing students to engage with material at deeper levels and develop problem-solving skills. It is well documented that teacher-dominated classes hinder student intellectual development (Boykin, 2000; Freire, 1972; Stanley & Noblit, 2009; Villegas & Lucas, 2007). It restricts the kind of out-of-the-box thinking that promotes innovation and progress and continues to promote powerlessness.

Even the identified "geniuses" have been taught within this limiting sphere of knowledge, which constricts their intellectual acumen and potential as well. The western conceptualization of intelligence has always been largely based in verbal skills (English proficiency) and logical-mathematical reasoning in order to produce if-then conveyor-belt–style thinkers in order to feed an industrial-based factory model of society (Li, 2002). Because the cultural foundation of western education has always been singularly focused, there has not been emic-level consideration of the fact that different cultures place value on different things as they pertain to educational attainment.

Thus, even though African American, Latinx, Indigenous American, and Asian youth were begrudgingly integrated into public schools at this point in time, the curricular content never shifted in order to include or consider them. They were thrown into a system that did not care about their needs because they did not want them there. These students were placed with teachers who did not like them and who were never trained to consider that cultural differences might play a role in the learning process.

Markus and Kitayama (1998) state that different cultures have very different understandings of the self and others and how these two ideas interact. These understandings also have great impact on cognition, emotion, and motivation (Boekaerts, 1998; Hammond, 2015; Markus & Kitayama, 1998; McIntyre, 1996). The fact that students perceive in culturally based ways alone can lead to students being weeded out as subpar simply because they are wired to think, process, and respond differently, and students who ascribe to the preferred view being raised up among the ranks of the "geniuses," further contributing to an ingrained and pervasive intellectual dichotomy.

Minor shifts in base views of intelligence at the etic level have occurred in conjunction with shifts in trends in education. For instance, the U.S. Space Race engendered a greater focus on scientific inquiry and innovation (Bybee & Fuchs, 2006). However, throughout the shifting trends, the basis of education has again remained the same and persisted.

We currently exist in a technologically advanced age, and yet technology has not been successfully integrated into schools that are not in affluent areas (Berk & Meyer, 2016; Washington, 2012). This is yet another marker of difference that preservice teachers were not taught to engage. In these areas, either there is a shortage of resources with a student to computer ratio of 20:1 or they do not exist due to lack of funding. I worked in one district where computers were shared among three schools.

The Commission on Excellence in Education declared in 1983 that the United States was a "nation at risk," identifying the educational system as mediocre and substandard (Ladson-Billings & Henry 1990). We are literally still using, and teachers are still required to enforce, the same educational structure. Recent research states that U.S. education is still in trouble as K–12 students cannot compete internationally and are not college ready upon graduation from this system (Boykin, 2000; Conley & Wise, 2011; Miller & Slocombe, 2012; National Assessment of Educational Progress, 2019).

American youth of all backgrounds are behind the curve. The current system continues to prepare them for an outdated nineteenth-century-based labor force instead of for the dynamic, globally based twenty-first-century collegiate-influenced system and workforce. Children in America are coming up in a diverse pluralistic world, yet diverse cultures are consistently left out of the educational equation both in the K–12 spectrum and in preservice teacher education (Berk & Meyer, 2016; Boykin, 2000; Jensen, 2003; Ladson-Billings, 2017; Li, 2002; Sefa Dei, 2008; Winter, 2000).

Half a century after desegregation, we are still experiencing separateness in U.S. schools in terms of socioeconomic distribution, which socially lends itself to race. This is complicated by unequal learning experiences both within schools and between schools (Tomlinson & Javius, 2012). Across the nation a plethora of public schools are poverty stricken and overwhelmingly populated by low-income and racially/linguistically diverse pupils.

They are also staffed with burned out, inexperienced, and emotionally disconnected teachers and administrators and saturated with outdated and poor-quality academic materials. Neighboring schools in better areas are attended by more affluent and privileged families. They also receive better funding and more qualified teachers (Berk & Meyer, 2016; National Center for Educational Statistics, 2016; Simon & Johnson, 2013; Singh, 2011; Tomlinson & Javius, 2012), although these experienced teachers are still not trained to be culturally competent.

Within schools, either students are tracked to intellectual paths (enrolled in International Baccalaureate, Advanced Placement, and/or Honors courses) or they are tracked toward technical paths where they are placed in remedial or easy courses (Cisneros et al., 2014; Irvine, 1990; Kanno & Kangas, 2014; Kohli, 2014). Students of color and lower socioeconomic status are more often tracked to the latter lane (Bailey & Paisley, 2004; Cokley, 2003, 2015; DeCuir-Gunby, 2009). This tracking is not based on ability.

Beyond this, at the individual state or school district level, English only and other harmful policies seek to explicitly exclude the heritage of students from the curriculum (Cabrera et al., 2014; Paris, 2012). For example, Arizona House Bill 2281 (2010), also known as the Ethnic Studies Ban, prohibits the study of the histories, heritage, and struggles of certain cultures in the public school system.

A school district or charter school in this state shall not include in its program of instruction any courses or classes that include any of the following:

1. Promote overthrow of the United States government.
2. Promote resentment toward a race or class of people.
3. Are designed primarily for pupils of a particular ethnic group.

4. Advocate ethnic solidarity instead of the treatment of pupils as individuals.

The local school board and the Arizona State Board of Education formulated this policy in order to close the Mexican American Studies (MAS) program in Tucson Unified School District (Cabrera et al., 2014; Paris, 2012). Administrative TUSD data from 2008–2011 assessed the relationship between taking MAS classes and passing the Arizona state standardized tests and high school graduation. Scores indicate that MAS students performed better on the AIMS (standardized test) and graduated at a higher rate than their White counterparts in the district.

This program was experiencing considerable success with educating Latinx students from their cultural frame of reference. The program employed texts that engaged youth in critical thinking about the interlocking themes of race and oppression. These youth were critically engaged with concepts that directly impact their well-being all while excelling academically, yet it was dismantled. The students were becoming too aware of societal inequities.

The bill is worded in a manner that implicitly excludes the cultural reality of diverse students as an option for future programmatic enhancement. Paris (2012) argues that such policies and practices are a return to the deficit perspective of old, and they allow for the system to be run as it is, ignoring the pluralistic reality of America. This creates pockets of powerlessness and lends to lower achievement motivation as diverse students confront the harsh reality of ethnicity-based disadvantages within the educational arena (Henfield & Washington, 2012; Li, 2002).

Because of this, the current structure of the American school system is flawed at the foundation level. It consistently creates and maintains opportunity gaps for students from underprivileged backgrounds throughout the structure (Milner, 2012; Irving & Hudley, 2008). This is unfortunately an enduring problem.

Challenges in the Current Educational Landscape

The National Assessment of Educational Progress, also known as the Nation's Report Card, tracks national scores for fourth- and eighth-grade mathematics and reading yearly as a way to keep track of national performance. The 2019 results indicate that although the gap is slightly lower than it has been in past years, there is still a consistent difference in scores. They reported a 25-point gap in scores for fourth-grade mathematics, 32-point gap for eighth-grade mathematics, 26-point gap for fourth-grade reading, and a 28-point gap for eighth-grade reading scores between White and Black students.

The score gaps for White versus Latinx students were 18, 24, 21, and 20 points respectively. The gaps for White versus Indigenous American students were 22, 30, 26, and 24. The score gaps for high- versus low-socioeconomic status were 24, 30, 28, and 25. Some teachers cited lack of resources as a contributing factor. Twelfth-grade reports were not available for 2019; however, 2015 scores indicate a similar trend with score gaps of 30 points for both reading and mathematics between White and Black Students, a 20- and 22-point gap for White and Latino students, and a 17- and 22-point gap in scores for White and Indigenous Americans students (National Assessment of Educational Progress, 2015).

The scores represented in the report incorporate students with disabilities, students living in poverty who are eligible for free and reduced lunch programs, as well as English language learners fitting within the prescribed ethnic categories. These numbers reflect a consistent gap in learning between the dominant culture and marginalized communities across the K–12 educational experience nationally. It also reflects back to the public school model of education originally proposed by Thomas Jefferson over two hundred years ago.

Upon consideration of these recent scores, the question becomes: Where do these challenges come from and what perpetuates them throughout the K–12 American educational journey of diverse students? Where do we begin to end disproportionate educational experiences in the United States? The sad reality is that America still relies on etic and critically outdated notions of what it means to learn and what it means to achieve and teachers are again still being "prepared" to perpetuate these outdated norms.

Ladson-Billings (2014) states that in order to answer these questions and shift toward making positive change at the student level, it makes sense to scrutinize the success of the marginalized group that consistently has been the least successful within the American educational system. She argues that gazing through this lens would provide a basis from which to begin, and it would divulge pedagogical pathways to optimal achievement for *all* students. African Americans are arguably the lowest performing marginalized group (Ladson-Billings, 2014; National Assessment of Educational Progress, 2015, 2019).

Ladson-Billings (2000) argues that the African American experience is unique partly because this is the only group that was transported to the United States against their will for the purposes of labor exploitation. To keep them in a space of servitude, a racial hierarchy and dichotomy was created that would continually transmit messages of inferiority and incapability that would in turn prompt parents to socialize African American youth to prepare them first to keep their heads down to avoid attention and later to stand tall in the face of bias (Hughes, 2003).

Their educational experience in America, which has been modeled after the values of the culture on the other end of the dichotomy (White students), has consistently mirrored this view, perpetuating low expectations and what Cokley (2015) calls the myth of Black anti-intellectualism. In this view, African-descent youth deign to achieve because success in the current educational system is synonymous with acting White or holding an outside cultural perspective as more salient than their own (Morris, 2008). Unfortunately, all of this is still relevant and reflected in the current 2017 national report card.

Snapshot of Marginalization: African American Community

Historically, African Americans have placed a vast amount of energy into educational attainment. For example, strong cultural affiliations within the group have been linked to having a strong value for learning and education (Allen & Boykin, 1992; Chavous et al., 2003). This energy and value is evidenced by enslaved Africans sneaking to learn how to read, freed Blacks establishing their own schools both formally and informally, and fighting against the idea of "separate but equal" by integrating schools in the attempt to attain equal and comparable education.

More recently, it has shown up in the creation of African-centered schools to center learning on Black students so that they do not have to fight the system or be socialized to think their culture has not made any significant contributions. Paradoxically, since desegregation, the African American school experience has been overwhelmingly characterized by

- high dropout rates, poor performance in courses, low test scores due to inappropriate instruction, and inappropriate assessment instruments (Griffin, 2002; Xu & Drame, 2008);
- overrepresentation in remedial and special education courses (Cartledge & Kourea, 2008; Crago et al., 1997; Harris-Murri, King, & Rostenberg, 2006; Kea & Utley, 1998; Klingner et al., 2005; Lomotey, 1992; McIntyre, 1996; Serpell et al., 2009; Xu & Drame, 2008);
- discriminatory discipline practices (Irvine, 1990; McIntyre, 1996; Smith & Harper, 2015; Win et al., 2011);
- a high rate of referrals into the criminal justice system (Ladson-Billings, 2014; Smith & Harper, 2015; Win et al., 2011); and

- underrepresentation or limited access to Gifted education, Advanced Placement, and International Baccalaureate courses (Bailey & Paisley, 2004; Cokley, 2003, 2015; DeCuir-Gunby, 2009).

This experience is partly due to the fact that culture has traditionally been ignored, misunderstood, or devalued in the American schools (Ali, Rohindra, & Coll, 2008; Arizona House Bill 2281, 2010; Kea & Utley, 1998; McCray, Grant, & Beachum, 2010; Singh, 2011). This is perpetuated because it has not yet been successfully integrated into teacher preparation programs in a meaningful or consistent way (Renner et al., 2004).

Jensen (2003) discusses cultural identity formation, stating that adolescents create multicultural identities because they grow up saturated in cultural beliefs and behaviors. Culture guides cognition (Hammond, 2015; McIntyre, 1996). So what happens when none of this is reflected in the curriculum? What message does it send when one perspective is singled out over all others? What does this communicate about worth and worthiness? What does this communicate about teachers' perceptions of these students?

This oversight has led to school failure. Students from marginalized backgrounds end up performing poorly on nationwide indicators of scholastic success (National Assessment of Educational Progress, 2019), developing a sense of "cultural mistrust" (Irving & Hudley, 2005), and becoming disconnected from the process. These reactions lead to disidentification with learning in general (Ali, Rohindra, & Coll, 2008; Cokley, 2002; Griffin, 2002; Osborne, 1997; Osborne, Walker, & Rausch, 2002), as well as missed opportunities to explore the implications of culture in the classroom.

According to Hilliard (1992), three clear problem areas exist in education that can be addressed and informed by what we know about how culture manifests in the classroom and mitigated by the way we train teachers to address culture. Misunderstandings of cultural behavioral styles, or cultural miscommunications between students and teachers, have been shown to lead to errors in the estimation of

1. intellectual potential, leading to mislabeling (ADHD, attention seeking, disruptive, emotional disturbances, mental retardation, socially maladaptive behaviors), misplacement in special education, and mistreatment of children (Crago et al., 1997; Gay, 2002; Hilliard, 1992);
2. learned abilities or achievement in academic subjects such as reading or math (perceived learning disabilities); and
3. language abilities (speech and language impairments).

McIntyre (1996) maintains that the very method in which educators teach, without the acknowledgment of cultural considerations, could very well be the cause of emotional and behavioral problems that arise in the classroom. These behavior problems get in the way of learning because they detract from lessons as teachers spend too much time reprimanding students rather than teaching content. The problem is that teachers are not connecting the behaviors to the content but instead attributing them to deficits in their students.

Differences in cultural behavioral styles are being interpreted by teachers as deficiencies, and a number of students are missing vital aspects of instruction due to classroom discipline that is in some cases unwarranted (Crago et al., 1997; Matthews et al., 2010; McIntyre, 1996; Smith & Harper, 2015; Xu & Drame, 2008). Crago et al. (1997) call this a lack of communicative competency, and Gay (2002) states that this stems from the "misunderstood incongruencies," or cultural mismatch, between home and school cultural standards rather than perceived "biological malfunctions" or intellectual limitations existing within the student.

Irvine (1990) and Crago et al. (1997) also discussed this notion of a conflict arising from cultural misunderstandings between teachers and their students. According to the authors, the disconnect develops when teachers of any background do not consider, acknowledge, or understand the cultural values, norms, communication patterns, and behavior styles their diverse students bring to the classroom. They also do not consider how these might conflict with the communicative competence needed to navigate the school system successfully (Cokley, 2015; Crago et al., 1997).

There is also a gender divide between the primarily female teaching force and male students. There is also a divide between middle-class teachers and students from differing socioeconomic backgrounds. Class creates differing sociocultural experiences, where teachers who have been raised in a higher socioeconomic space, even if they are the same ethnicity, can find student language and behavior difficult to decipher. They are finding it difficult to connect.

This topic is salient because cultural misunderstandings between students and teachers can have severe consequences on student outcomes. These incongruences lead to unbalanced and discriminatory discipline practices in school settings due to an imbalance of power that exists between teachers and administrators who are the authorities and students who have no say in the situation. For instance, recent research has shown that Black students continue to be suspended and expelled from school and referred to the criminal justice system at disproportionately high rates compared to students from other backgrounds (Crago et al., 1997; Hammond, 2015; Renner et al. 2004; Smith & Harper, 2015).

Power differentials are compounded by dissimilarities in culture, gender, and socioeconomic status. At times students from marginalized backgrounds have even been found to receive harsher punishments than White students committing the exact same offense. This is an issue that has been circulating the literature for over three decades without resolution. This could very well be mitigated through teacher preparation. All of this could be addressed by focusing on understanding of and comfort with culture, gender, and socioeconomic status during teacher preparation.

Through these "misunderstood incongruencies" the school setting can appear to be very oppositional to the home and community culture of students of African descent. The system is asking them to be something they are not seven hours out of the day while discounting their identities. This causes feelings of dis-ease (Allen & Boykin, 1992; Butler, 2003; Grills, 2002; Howard, 2002).

These contradictions can appear in the form of independent and competitive forms of learning and achievement. Students are required to work individually on assignments that do not hold any meaning for them or compete with one another for points and/or the highest grade (Butler, 2003; Bruning et al., 2004). This contributes to a dualistic nature and requires the student to know how to code switch efficiently in order to successfully navigate the school system.

Fordham and Ogbu (1986) maintained that the African American experience with having to code switch and give up a piece of their identity in order to succeed nurtured an "oppositional and collective cultural identity" whereby to be authentically Black requires the rejection of anything that promotes White cultural values and norms. This theory of oppositional identity gave rise to the myth that achieving is antithetical to being Black. Whereas Cokley (2015) acknowledges that this may be a consideration for the performance of some students, he explains that this is not the norm for all students of African descent.

It also does not hold accountable the inadequate school system or inadequate teacher preparation, both of which are failing these students on a large scale. Over the past twenty-five years, many scholars have stated that the answer to navigating these problematic educational spaces is to leave them. Some are choosing to resegregate and to create and sustain African-centered schools rather than continue to subject students to a school system in which they are not considered or even ignored (Boykin, 2000; Cokley, 2003, 2015; Durden, 2007; Irvine, 1990; Kea & Utley, 1998; Lee, Lomotey,

& Shujaa 1990; Lomotey, 1992; Merry & New, 2008; Murrell, 2002; Rivers & Rivers, 2002).

Many of these schools are empirically effective in teaching, nurturing, and enhancing the academic identification of students from this community (Black Star Educational Institute, 2020; Imhotep Academy, 2017; Teicher, 2006). This is absolutely an ideal space for many African-descent families in America; however, not everyone can afford the private school tuition that it takes to run such institutions, and a number of parents do not have access to the information about these spaces, thus urban school districts are over-populated with African American children. This, then, is where the work must be done.

According to *The Condition of Education* (2016) report by the National Center for Educational Statistics, a higher percentage of not only Black (45 percent) students but also Latinx (45 percent) and Indigenous (36 percent) students were found to be living in poverty and attending high-poverty/impoverished public schools. Where the American educational system as a whole has been labeled as mediocre, schools serving the needs of impoverished communities face additional challenges to achievement (Boykin, 2000; Ladson-Billings & Henry, 1990).

It is time to revamp the educational landscape for students of diverse backgrounds by creating a culturally sustaining educational context (Durden, 2008; Hughes, 2003; Xu & Drame, 2008). This will happen only when we rewrite the rules to the game. Teacher education must lead the charge to produce educators who can lead the way in enhancing the curriculum of the U.S. educational system, reflecting the pluralistic nature of America in order to enhance the experiences of *all* students within public schools as well as overall academic and psychological outcomes.

A First-Person Side Note on Teacher Burnout

Think back to the quote at the beginning of chapter 1 that mentioned teachers having to labor through the system. Many of them feel as though they are enduring it along with the students. This chapter has explained what is happening in classrooms across the country in terms of student experiences. There are always three sides to a story, what one person sees, what the other person sees, and what is really going on. So how is all of this affecting the teachers?

One account comes from a local elementary school as the researcher was working with third- through fifth-graders to prepare them for the state writing exam. Traversing the halls collecting students for the sessions, one could witness various indices of teachers who are just plain unhappy, apathetic, and burned out. In one classroom the teacher literally yelled in the face of a student who was not moving fast enough for her.

Her face was about three inches away from his. Is this not textbook bullying behavior? She was so engrossed in her irritation that she did not see how his face fell and she unknowingly flipped the switch on his disengagement. She also did not see how she was modeling this behavior for her students.

In another room, the teacher asked the researcher for a description of what she was doing with students at the school. Once she explained that she was in essence a writing coach, he responded by saying, "I need to find out how to do that because I cannot continue to do this" as he gestured toward his students. They being the *this* he was referring to. Again, he did not see their faces at this dismissal of their individual value to him as their daytime guardian.

As the researcher quietly and discreetly asked another teacher for the next student group, she yelled out, "Who are my low people?" She then proceeded to call student names out, connecting them to that horrible identifier. One of the students walked over and sadly asked, "Am I low?"

The researcher had to bend down, comfort her, and explain that she was absolutely *not* low. The message was punctuated with a hug, and then the entirety of the lesson was spent showing her and the other students who were called out by this teacher how much they already knew and how well they were doing. She had them provide examples for concepts from their prior knowledge and had them do fun demonstrations where they were teaching the content to one another.

Another teacher was so convinced that her student was "lazy and just does not want to do anything" that she would not listen when the researcher attempted to explain that he is not lazy but rather in need of help. She had to be shown how his behavior was not disruptive or intended to be disrespectful but that it was indicative of a student who needed help reading and comprehending the passage so that he could even be able to write a response essay. She was eventually able to hear the concern and accept the differing perspective on the underlying basis of his behavior.

Each of these situations was painful. The researcher did her best to mitigate the emotional impact on the students who most definitely felt disliked, defeated, and unimportant. These are in fact just a tiny example of the multiple scenarios witnessed in various schools in many different districts.

Many of these teachers are in crisis. Many of them post consistently about hating Mondays, asking on Tuesday if it is Friday yet, fighting through hump day Wednesday, and thanking God it's Friday. Some take as many "sick" days as humanly and HR-ly possible. Some show up every day and wear their unhappiness on their faces and their sleeves. How exactly do they get to this point?

According to the research, novice teachers are often given posts at schools and with children who are considered to be difficult. The lack of a global perspective can help to foster negative views of these students and this community. Couple this with a perceived lack of support from administration, disconnection from parents, and student behaviors in response to disidentification and unfair schooling practices and the perfect storm is created. Consider the following personal account from a past student of mine who stopped teaching after three years in the classroom:

Teaching wasn't something that I wanted to do since I was a kid. It found me and I loved every second that I was able to actively be engaged in changing my students' lives directly and indirectly, whether it was helping them understand a new concept or overcoming a barrier in their life. I left teaching to fulfill a dream of being a nurse, but other factors helped make my decision to leave education easier.

1. Lack of Support from Administration
We all have a job to do within a business. After year two, I felt that administration did not have my best interest or that of ALL of my students at heart. It often felt like an uphill battle and I received little support when dealing with difficult parents. I was often overlooked when interested in positions of leadership and advancement of my skill set. It was more of a popularity contest than it was about focusing on the education of the kids. I was constantly micromanaged to make sure I was catering to a specific group of parents. It was tiring and discouraging. My level of intellect was challenged constantly, and I was expected to work miracles on students with behavior issues because "I got them" and "they" could relate with "me."

2. Overall Burnout
I found myself spending more hours at the school than I was paid for; volunteering, grading papers, tutoring, remediating, enriching, attending professional development meetings, and so much more. I was tired! I was tired of being the first person there and the last to leave. I was tired of fighting for my students and advocating for them with no backing or being told, "that's just the way things were." I was tired of being the ONLY source of motivation for my students. I was tired of jumping through hoops to make the impossible happen. I was tired of being the ONLY person who wanted more. I was mentally, emotionally, and just physically tired. I dreaded getting up most mornings.

This account gets to the heart of the problem as it pertains to teachers as well as to the heart of the underlying message of this book. When speaking of changing the game, this means that teachers and the system are capable of doing so much better. The children deserve so much better. An entire overhaul of the system is needed.

When teacher education shifts to include celebration of multiple and global perspectives, all preservice teachers and future educational leaders who are funneled into the system will be able to see these issues from a different perspective. They will have an intricate understanding of the harm it is causing. There will be more than just one or a few advocates in a particular school. There will be more professionals at multiple levels focused on changing, updating, diversifying, and energizing the curriculum because that is what needs to happen to ensure the success of *all* students. Change the game by changing the players, by effecting change within. The apples need to be figuratively replaced with capes.

CHAPTER THREE

~

Why Context Matters!

Empathy isn't just listening, it's asking the questions whose answers need to be listened to. Empathy requires inquiry as much as imagination. Empathy requires knowing you know nothing. Empathy means acknowledging a horizon of context that extends perpetually beyond what you can see.

—Leslie Jamison

Introduction

In a pluralistic society, it should go without saying that all students, regardless of socioeconomic status or cultural background, deserve access to education that is challenging, appropriate, equitable, engaging, and robust. The only way to change the game and transform school into an equitable (not equal because this means something entirely different) experience is to include the stories and cultural realities of every pupil, making teachers communicatively competent across cultural categories. This would be a step in removing the culturally imperialistic foci of perpetuating majority culture as the norm against which all else is measured and found wanting (Crago et al., 1997; Tomlinson & Javius, 2012; Young, 2004).

Twenty-four years ago, Gloria Ladson-Billings (1995a) introduced the idea of a model of education that would honor the lived experience of marginalized learners alongside that of the majority (Thompson, 2015a; Ladson-Billings, 2014; Paris, 2012). She veered away from popular deficit deficiency models of education popular during this time, which focused on problems and perpetuated a negative view of these communities. Instead she asked the opposite question of what was *right* with African American learners.

Educational and psychological research and practice during the 1960s and 1970s were characterized by models and scholarship that viewed, and ultimately defined, the language, cultural practices, and knowledge base of various communities of color as deficient and problematic systems that needed to be fixed (Paris, 2012). These communities were labeled as *culturally disadvantaged* or *culturally deprived* because they did not mirror the ideas and views of the dominant White culture, which again permeated the American school system as well as the psychological community in terms of what was deemed acceptable, optimal, and *normal* (Paris, 2012). The "culture of poverty" research was born, and anything on the outside of this acceptable box was deemed abnormal and in need of culturally imposed intervention.

This also led to the creation of deficit models and the misguided rationale for Indian boarding schools. Indigenous children were taken away from their families and stripped of their name, culture, and Indigenous language and spirituality for the purpose of "cultural enhancement" as they were deemed culturally bankrupt (Bennett, 2015; Paris, 2012). This process caused permanent damage to that community.

The Case for Culturally Relevant Pedagogy

Moving away from this school of thought, a number of resource pedagogies arose through the 1970s stretching into the 1990s aimed at the intersection of literacy/pedagogy, culture, and language in traditionally marginalized communities, namely African American, Asian American, Indigenous, Latinx, and Pacific Islander (Paris, 2012). Ladson-Billings (1995b) provided a name, context, and direction for the growing body of research. Culturally relevant pedagogy (CRP) became one of the most popular and enduring conceptualizations of those models.

In its multiple iterations, CRP has also come to be called culturally responsive pedagogy (Caszden & Leggett, 1976; Gay, 2002), culturally appropriate pedagogy (Au & Jordan, 1981), culturally compatible instruction (Jordan, 1985; Vogt, Jordan, & Tharp, 1987), culturally congruent pedagogy (Au & Kawakami, 1994; Mohatt & Erickson, 1981), and now culturally sustaining pedagogy (Ladson-Billings, 2017; McCarty & Lee, 2014; Paris, 2012). Regardless of nomenclature, the goal of this new pedagogy was to create a program that effectively put theory into practice. It would address the scholarship-practice gap by creating a paradigm that could not only be effectively carried out in one setting but also be replicated in order to change the educational landscape (Ball, 2012; DeAngelis, 2010; Ladson-Billings, 1995b; Singh, 2011).

Gloria Ladson-Billings (1995b) envisioned a pedagogical entity that would encompass culture (across categorical differences), pathways toward achievement for all students, and social justice or sociopolitical consciousness. This pedagogy would ultimately "produce students who can achieve academically, produce students who demonstrate cultural competence, and develop students who can both understand and," more importantly, "critique the existing social order" (p. 474). She wanted students to have "the ability to take learning beyond the confines of the classroom using school knowledge and skills to identify, analyze, and solve real-world problems" (Ladson-Billings, 2014, p. 75).

The main driving force behind culturally relevant pedagogy in its original form is the ability of teachers to connect learning ideologies with a richer understanding through an appreciation for culture (Ladson-Billings, 2014). It is predicated on the idea of first empowering students by acknowledging their cultural norms, focusing on their potential, and nurturing them to become leaders who are intellectually stimulating, emotionally competent, politically educated, and socioeconomically aware by introducing and presenting scholarly information through multiple lenses (Thompson, 2015a).

More specifically, Gay (2010) described the process of being culturally relevant or responsive (in one of the theory's other many forms) as encompassing five components.

Cultural Relevance Checklist (Excerpted from Gay [2010, p. 29])

✓ It acknowledges the legitimacy of the cultural heritages of different ethnic groups, both as legacies that affect students' dispositions, attitudes, and approaches to learning and as worthy content to be taught in the formal curriculum.

✓ It builds bridges of meaningfulness between home and school experiences as well as between academic abstractions and lived sociocultural realities.

✓ It uses a wide variety of instructional strategies that are connected to different learning styles.

✓ It teaches students to know and praise their own and each other's cultural heritages.

✓ It incorporates multicultural information, resources, and materials in all the subjects and skills routinely taught in schools.

CRP changes the educational conversation from cultural eradication and cultural assimilation into majority beliefs and behavioral ways of being to a discourse predicated on cultural competence (Ladson-Billings, 2014). This enriches content and assists students in making information meaningful in order to encode it and process it at deeper levels. In addition to this, teachers who are culturally responsive embrace the following traits and practices (Hsaio, 2015; Ladson-Billings, 2014):

Culturally Responsive Teacher Checklist

✓ They are socioculturally conscious.
✓ They appreciate diversity.
✓ They (continuously) participate in the process of challenging their own internal biases.
✓ They see themselves as cultural brokers in educational institutions.
✓ They understand and embrace constructivist views of knowledge, teaching, and learning.
✓ They learn about and know the lives of their students.
✓ They identify students' needs.
✓ They communicate with students and parents.
✓ They design instruction to draw on students' strengths and to address their needs.
✓ They design and implement curricula creating a caring and supporting setting.
✓ They deliver culturally responsive instruction.
✓ They enrich students' diverse cultures.

Understanding how the brain works and how learning happens, these teachers also acknowledge culturally responsive brain rules that connect not only to the learning process but also to how people make connections or create fissures in relating to others. Hammond (2015) identifies six principles that work together to interpret threats or opportunities:

1. The brain seeks to minimize social threats and maximize opportunities to connect with others in the community. If others are perceived to be threats to social or psychological well-being, the brain prompts the person to protect themselves.
2. Positive relationships keep our safety-threat detection system in check.

3. Culture guides how we process information.
4. Attention drives learning.
5. All new information must be coupled with existing funds of knowledge.
6. The brain physically grows through challenge and stretch, expanding its ability to do more complex thinking and learning.

The student and reaching her or his optimal level of functioning is the focus absent of harmful political agendas situated within a frame of social justice. In order to achieve this, these individuals must be willing to challenge and shed the veil of their own potentially harmful beliefs in order to incorporate the possibility that the cultural ways of being of others are valid and real. She or he would also have to understand that this acknowledgment does not negate or counter her or his own beliefs.

It would simply validate the existence of their students. However, this is not something that develops overnight. This is a continual process preservice, novice, and veteran teachers must go through in order to change the educational trajectory of marginalized students and nurture understanding and global knowledge in White students. This presents important implications for teacher education programs as well as the continued professional development of veteran teachers as student populations are constantly changing and transforming culturally.

Implications of accepting such a multifaceted pedagogical idea would mean a shift in traditional sociopolitical and sociohistorical power dynamics as once again the school microculture impacts and feeds the societal macroculture (Gregorčič, 2009). Dr. Wade Nobles has defined power as "the ability to create one's own definition of reality and have others respond to that definition as if it were their own." The U.S. school curriculum did not originally integrate along with the physical school spaces because the focus of teachers and administrators, as well as policy makers at that time, was not on welcoming and empowering all students.

The focus was to perpetuate and maintain the superiority of White students and White culture, beliefs, and attitudes through the process of acculturation (Bennet, 2015; Boykin, 2000; Young, 2004). Some might argue that desegregation, which was implemented in 1954 through the *Brown vs. the Board of Education* decision, was actually harmful and inequitable. The curriculum was never altered to incorporate the experiences or reality of children of African, Asian, Latino, or Indigenous descent and contributed to the Whitening of the teaching force and the curriculum (Morris, 2008; Sleeter, 2008).

This is where the monocultural school structure began. Desegregation was socially progressive yet in many ways educationally detrimental. St. John (1975) found that desegregation lowered the self-esteem and stunted the educational/vocational goals of African American children rather than placing them in a better position for achievement. There is no point in time when children of African descent were not problematized within this context.

Since the inception of the educational system, students have been acculturated or socialized to accept this monocultural reality as the norm and either adapt to it in order to achieve success or experience failure (Bailey & Paisley, 2004; Sleeter, 2008). The lens through which information is disseminated has not been adjusted. Thus, complete acceptance of this culturally infused pedagogy would prompt a shift in power from the majority group to balancing it out between all cultures that exist within American borders (responding to their own respective realities as valid and legitimate).

This more accurately represents what it means to be a valued participant in a democratic and pluralistic society. So what could this egalitarian culturally defined pedagogical reality look like? As CRP was introduced twenty-four years ago, the literature is rife with a number of independently successful programs created to test the efficacy of the theory and exemplify the success traditionally marginalized students would achieve if CRP were to be implemented in the national curriculum (Hanley & Noblit, 2009).

For instance, Ladson-Billings (1995a, 1995b) studied teacher influence on student outcomes. She found that their conception of self, ethic of care, and clear and deliberate curricular focus were important to academic success with diverse students, not just Black students. Again, she began with studying African American students to examine avenues to achievement for all students because they have historically presented as the lowest achieving group.

Ferguson (2002) conducted a study of ninety-five diverse schools in fifteen districts. The researcher found that teachers' affective behaviors motivate and positively impact academic achievement of African American and Latinx youth. Nasir (2002) reported similar results, finding that the link between cultural identity and schooling was integral to mathematics proficiency for African American adolescents.

Conrad, Gong, Sipp, and Wright (2004) coupled CRP with Text Talk to foster oral language skills and comprehension in elementary students, which was found to positively support literacy. The youth were exposed to cultural literature, connecting them personally to the texts. Students were able to give lengthy, in-depth answers when teachers set high expectations.

Moses-Snipes (2005) conducted a study implementing ethnomathematics and multicultural mathematics activities with fifth-grade African American students. Research found that achievement scores increased from pretest to posttest as they learned about African culture in conjunction with the math curriculum. Similarly, Lee (2006) successfully employed African American English (AAE) to teach complex literary reasoning, using language as a liberatory tool to make information more meaningful for participants.

The rhetorical language features of African American language provided context for comprehension for youth. Participants demonstrated competency in canonical text as connections were made to prior everyday knowledge utilizing AAE as the conduit. What was originally perceived as obtuse text was made understandable, meaningful, and relevant to the participants.

The idea of sharing power with students was presented by Cammarota and Romero (2009). They presented participatory action research that was conducted by their Latinx students. The study found that a rigorous curriculum aligned with state standards, combined with cultural content and authentic caring and compassion from teachers, increased student achievement and the graduation rate. This reflects the importance of the role of the teacher in student outcomes.

Kana'iaupuni, Ledward, and Jensen (2010) conducted a large-scale empirical study with Culture Based Education (CBE) in Hawaii with 600 teachers, 2,969 students, and 2,264 parents at 62 different schools. Students of CBE teachers reported higher rates of Hawaiian cultural affiliation ($p<.001$), community attachment ($p<.001$), greater school motivation and engagement ($p<.05$), higher levels of socioemotional development, and also a greater connection to and understanding of local issues. The students felt uniquely connected to the content.

In yet another successful example, Wu (2011) discusses the implementation of CRP in Chinese heritage language classrooms. This practice lays a foundation for liberatory culturally based literacy in the American education system. Emergent themes from the study were motivational skill building, integrating culture, and sharing power with students. Power keeps resurfacing as a salient aspect of success for students of color.

Worthy, Consalvo, Bogard, and Russell (2012) empowered students with negative reputations by "restorying" them. They employed culturally responsive instruction and the ethic of care by implementing personalized instruction and attention, classroom structure and curriculum, and socially based classroom interaction. Lastly, Paris (2012) and Cabrera et al. (2014) discuss the Mexican American Studies Program, which was shut down by the Tucson Unified School District, stating that this was an exemplary model of what CRP should be.

Another positive aspect of cultural competence/relevance is that it has the potential to increase family buy-in and involvement in the classroom, which has been shown to positively impact student achievement and outcomes (Kalyanpur & Harry, 1997). There is an adequate amount of empirical evidence here to show that CRP is successful in enhancing both the resilience and academic achievement of students from marginalized backgrounds (Hanley & Noblit, 2009). Most of the literature on CRP is presented from the perspective of researchers and program developers explaining the impact their respective studies had on students from marginalized backgrounds.

It is important to explore student perceptions of CRP as we examine favorable outcomes and discuss student empowerment (Hughes, Page, & Ford, 2011). Howard (2001) presents student responses indicating that the introduction of CRP made the content more engaging and made them want to apply the necessary effort to complete tasks. These students also called for "teachers who displayed caring bonds and attitudes toward them, teachers who established community- and family-type classroom environments, and teachers who made learning an entertaining and fun process" (p. 131).

The youth are calling for teachers who see them, who care about them, and who incorporate multiple perspectives. This is significant given the student experience discussed in chapter 2 in relation to teacher burnout and student disidentification. Each of the aforementioned studies presents favorable and positive outcomes for the youth involved in the research. The issue is that although there are successful examples of how to implement a culturally infused pedagogy, none of them has been enduring or attempted on a large scale and all of them have been incorporated into existing classroom environments as add-on interventions.

These interventions phase out after the culmination of the study and classrooms return to business as usual. Castagno and Brayboy (2008) state that schools are still failing to meet the needs of Indigenous students even though culturally relevant and responsive programs have been advocated in the literature for over forty years. They purport that this is partly due to culturally infused pedagogies being reduced to meaningless generalizations and surface-level presentations of what culture means that do not effect widespread systemic change.

It is also because preservice teachers are not being adequately prepared to acknowledge or integrate culture into the curricula in any meaningful way (Castagno & Brayboy, 2008; Hsaio, 2015; Ladson-Billings, 2017; Renner et al., 2014; Zhao, Meyers, & Meyers, 2009). Those who singularly attempt to practice are often not supported by administration. One could only imagine the outcomes if these successful programs were implemented at the inception of the school year, integrated into the classroom community structure and practices, and ongoing throughout the year.

There is a need for a curriculum to be created that could transcend categories and sustain through shifting dynamics in education with an emphasis on sovereignty and empowerment (Castagno & Brayboy, 2008; Ladson-Billings, 2014; McCarty & Lee, 2014). Teachers must also be adequately prepared to meet the challenge of implementation (Castagno & Brayboy, 2008; Zhao, Meyers, & Meyers, 2009). An additional focus of curricular change is trusting teachers to create engaging lessons and elicit student learning.

Toward a Culturally Sustaining Pedagogy

Though there have been some successful models of cultural relevance or responsivity, Ladson-Billings (2014) states that CRP has also been misused, misapplied, and mislabeled over the years, reduced to "the idea that adding some books about people of color, having a classroom Kwanzaa celebration, or posting 'diverse' images makes one 'culturally relevant'" (p. 82). Each of these things is a superficial manifestation of cultural acknowledgment and does not add to a deeper level of cultural understanding. The author discusses her struggle with the inability to maintain and control the very meaning of a concept she was instrumental in creating once it transmutes to the classroom through the individual teacher.

She thus calls for a remix of the theory. This reworking would honor the original purpose set forth in 1995 while acknowledging that change is constant within the educational sector as well as within individuals and cultural spaces. Ladson-Billings (2014) agrees with Paris (2012) that CRP should do what problematic curricula has not and grow with the times, shifting from what they describe as the "golden age" to an updated and dynamic model of culturally sustaining pedagogy (CSP).

This new model would also factor in the recent research focus on teachers working to create critical thinking, global-minded citizens (Ali, Rohindra, & Coll, 2008; Agbaria, 2011; Miller & Slocombe, 2012). A specific focus on sociopolitical dimensions of education would need to be added in as well. They have been traditionally glossed over, viewed through the prism of Whiteness, or altogether omitted from CRP models.

As society shifts, so too does the "culture of power" moving away from Whiteness. Thus, this perspective would incorporate student advocacy and the scrutiny of policies that directly affect students, schools, and the larger community (Ladson-Billings, 2014; Paris, 2012; Paris & Alim, 2014; Renner et al., 2004). This is vital as Villegas and Lucas (2007) state that the process of learning involves teachers guiding students through "questioning, interpreting, and analyzing ideas in the context of meaningful issues" (p. 2).

Paris and Alim (2014) explain that the word *relevance* was not a strong enough term to reflect the goals of CRP and does not necessarily support dynamic continuity in learning and practice. Thus, the name needed to transform in order to reflect the multifaceted and dynamic aim of the concept. The goal through CSP is to create a pedagogical system that is culturally informed, relevant, student specific, dynamic, linguistically centered, politically charged, and above all sustainable through time, across space, context, and experience.

This system would be led by educators who are culturally receptive, competent, and open to continued growth, understanding that the system would continue to flow with time and through encounters with new students and colleagues. This process, which should be instilled through teacher education programs (Ladson-Billings, 2014), would promote multiculturalism and multilingualism by employing paths specific to each cultural community and revitalizing lost or ignored languages (McCarty & Lee, 2014). For example, cultural sustainability for Indigenous communities would have to include revitalization in order to restore the language and culture that has been stripped away for generations.

Language in general is a salient aspect of "cultural continuity and community sustainability because it embodies both everyday and sacred knowledge and is essential to ceremonial practice" (McCarty & Lee, 2014). The words needed to engage in spiritual practice may not exist in English, thus returning the language to the people and using it to teach allows them a deeper level of cultural immersion and a greater sense of both personal and cultural empowerment. The United Nations Educational, Scientific, and Cultural Organization published a paper speaking to this very issue back in 1953, which was actually predesegregation. *The Use of Vernacular Languages in Education* stated:

> On educational grounds we recommend that the mother tongue be extended to as late a stage in education as possible. In particular pupils should begin their schooling through the medium of the mother tongue, because they understand it best and because to begin their school life in the mother tongue will make the break between home and school as small as possible. . . . We consider that the shock which the young child undergoes in passing from his home to his school life is so great that everything possible should be done to soften it. . . . The use of the mother-tongue will promote better understanding between the home and school.

Now sixty-six years later, the United States is still attempting to mitigate the effects of ignoring the recommendations in this report.

In addition to linguistic sovereignty, CSP will also be built on the ideas of pluralism and empowerment. Teachers would be expected to balance what Ladson-Billings (2014) refers to as a dual responsibility of managing external performance assessments while maintaining a student/community-centered focus on learning. In this context students will be able to honor their origins or personal/group heritage, including a pointed emphasis on language maintenance (McCarty & Lee, 2014; Singh, 2011), while also being able to incorporate the dominant perspective (Castagno & Brayboy, 2008).

That is, once the dominant educational perspective is modified and enhanced to remove biases often found in curricular resources, which indirectly harm marginalized students. For instance, Grant and Gillespie (1993) presented a list of ten biases that have been permeating educational texts and materials since the inception of the American educational system. These biases both advertently and inadvertently promote the superiority of a singular view and negate the contributions diverse cultures have made globally.

Biases Permeating Educational Materials
(From Grant & Gillespie [1993, pp. 17–19])

1. Bias by omission: selecting information that reflects credit on only one group, frequently the writer's or speaker's group.
2. Bias by defamation: calling attention to the Native person's faults rather than virtues and misrepresenting the nature of Native people.
3. Bias by disparagement: denying or belittling the contribution of Native people to mainstream culture.
4. Bias by cumulative implication: constantly creating the impression that only one group is responsible for positive development.
5. Bias by (lack of) validity: failing to ensure that information about issues is accurate and unambiguous.
6. Bias by inertia: perpetuation of legends and half-truths by failure to keep abreast of historical scholarship.
7. Bias by obliteration: ignoring significant aspects of Indigenous history.

8. Bias by disembodiment: referring in a causal and depersonalized way to a group of people.
9. Bias by (lack of) concreteness: dealing with a race or group in generalizations that apply shortcomings, or positive characteristics, of one individual to the group. To be concrete, the material must be factual, objective, and realistic.
10. Bias by (lack of) comprehensiveness and balance: failure to mention all relevant facts that may help form student opinions.

This list reflects bias toward the Indigenous population; however, unfortunately many of the points can easily be generalized to other marginalized communities. This continued practice is at the root of marginalization and can be mitigated by correctly infusing CSP in teacher education programs. Educators focused on cultural sustainability would recognize these biases and block them from harming their students.

Initiating a curricular overhaul in which disenfranchised communities are able to participate and merging it with culturally sustaining practice would create a multicultural/ antiracist and emancipatory education. School could be transformed into a sovereign and empowering space as it makes room for the possibility and inclusion of multiple truths (Irving & Hudley, 2008; Paris, 2012; Renner et al., 2004; Singh, 2011). This would allow youth the ability to be nurtured within their own frame of reference and be academically competitive, meeting approved national standards (Castagno & Brayboy, 2008; Ladson-Billings, 2014; Paris, 2012; Sefa Dei, 2008).

A correctly implemented CSP would embrace and enhance national educational standards yet redirect the singular focus on teaching to tests. The focus is on student learning and growth. Both perspectives must be incorporated and honored in order to nurture balanced, healthy, and successful outcomes for all students. This is the game changer that will transform schooling into an experience where both teachers and students enjoy the process and thrive with no exceptions.

~

CHAPTER FOUR

Sawubona . . . We See You!

Teaching anywhere is difficult if the teacher perceives his pupils a "they." One interesting and reliable index of a volunteer's community involvement is the language he uses to describe the community. Generally, the use of such terms as "these people," "the natives," "them," "they," and "theirs" indicates superficial community contact; the use of terms such as "our town," "my pupils," and "our school" indicates a more intimate involvement.

—Asa Hilliard, 1967, p. 35

I've learned that people will forget what you said, people will forget what you did, but people will never forget how you made them feel.

—Maya Angelou

Introduction

In the Zulu culture, people greet each other by saying sawubona. This greeting goes much deeper than simply saying hello or an empty "how are you doing" that is not really asking for a response regarding the person's wellbeing. The translation of this word from isiZulu into English would be "we see you," meaning I and the ancestors that walk with me acknowledge you and your lineage.

This greeting acknowledges the essence of the person and reinforces the understanding that they belong to a community of people who literally feel their presence. They are not invisible or extraneous. Their deep importance is communicated to them in one word. The plural greeting to more than one person is sanibonani, communicating the same thing to the group. Each of you is seen and felt.

This beautiful and multilayered greeting taps into the importance and benefits of being seen and acknowledged by others. It also highlights why it is imperative to be understood by the person seeing you. Claude Steel introduced the fear many students of color have of being viewed negatively through the guise of stereotype and identified as lacking. The focus here is on the desire to be positively seen and accepted.

The Power of Being Attended To

When attention is positive, the beautiful feeling attached to this recognition is almost indescribable. It feels good. It makes people want to be connected to the person who sees them. When that person is a teacher, it generates a deeper level of respect and it makes one want to put forth one's best effort in class. It makes a person feel as though they can do anything.

At the very foundation, humans are social to the core because people exist within the context of others from conception. The Kikuyu people of Kenya say "umuntu ngumuntu, ngabantu," meaning "a person is a person because we are people." Individuals remain in the charge of others with varying degrees of independence, though still very much in connection, until they are eighteen (nineteen in some states like Nebraska) or considered to be grown in socially prescribed terms.

Even when we are grown, we thrive in relationship with others through physical touch and through consideration. This constant connection with others manifests as the desire to seek the attention and approval of adults who are in charge of our development. To be invisible to these adults is to feel alone and unimportant, and it can interrupt development, create feelings of alienation, and devolve into hopelessness at the extreme.

Paying close attention, it is possible to see a spark die in someone's eyes when they feel invisible and misunderstood. There is almost a visible deflation. This othering process, discussed by Hilliard (1967), sends clear communication that the person sees no value in the students, in their community (which is a piece of who they are), or in the space they are occupying in students' lives. This can be very isolating, and it can be very painful to experience.

Isolation is an anomaly as it pertains to the human condition and carries with it grave psychological and emotional implications in terms of optimal functioning. If we connect this conversation to the concept of neglect in parenting theory, the adverse outcomes to disconnection reflect current issues in education for marginalized youth. Students who find themselves in the margins in the American education system can become emotionally withdrawn and disidentify with schooling. They can rebel by acting out behaviorally, and they can experience anxiety and fear, exhibiting stress responses leading toward academic failure.

Student-Teacher Relationships

The research on student-teacher relationships is clear in regard to the benefits of teachers forming meaningful connections with their students. These connections cannot manifest without an understanding of who students are and all the potential they bring with them to the classroom. That understanding begins with getting to know students, where they are from (both culturally and geographically), and what is important to them.

The Canorous Case of Mr. Halvorson presented in the introduction to this book provides a practical and tangible example of how that educator transformed the school experience for every single one of the diverse students who crossed his path. They were clear in his interactions with them that he not only saw their humanity but also felt it and connected with it. All students were clear that they, their backgrounds, and their perspectives were valued.

That knowledge was empowering and it freed them, allowing them to tap into the content in deeper ways. His gaze allowed for students to be able to play within the content and to create within their level of understanding, translating into drawing deeper connections. These students learned to engage and analyze differently because he saw them and never let them forget it.

Another example of the importance of being seen comes from listening to a personal account from the author's daughter discussing her schooling experiences with teachers over the years. Remember that teachers have the power to connect or disconnect. They have the power to engage or disengage. They have the power to subjugate or free. This young lady is an avid learner, much like her mother, who also embodies the same love of books. She devours up to three leisure books per week (much to the chagrin of her mother's bank account) in addition to the work she is doing for school and the clubs she belongs to.

She was always excited about learning new things and about simply going to school until she advanced to middle school. Here she experienced a few teachers who did not take the time to get to know the students and really see and know them individually. This self-learner who loved engaging with every subject (with a special shout out to reading and math) began to say that she disliked going to math or some of her other classes.

Her complaints were never about the content but about the treatment from (or the ignoring by) the teacher. Teachers who focused more on the students who were misbehaving and punished *all* students together for the transgressions of a few. Teachers who did not allow their students to have a voice. Witnessing this shift and hearing her say things like "why isn't learning fun anymore," "it doesn't matter because they don't listen to what we have to say," or "s/he does not care about my life" was very painful both as a mother and as an educator. All of the implications inherent in these statements were blaringly loud.

She was beginning to disengage. She did not see the ability to express her view or advocate for herself with her teachers. Yes, she was partly joking when she said the last statement about them not caring about her life, but she was also (very) seriously saying that these teachers did not see her. They did not see the curious, considerate, passionate, scientific, deep thinker that her parents and past teachers saw when marveling at her brain and the connections she makes in conversation.

They were not listening for her voice and amplifying it. They did not see her heart. They were not furthering, inspiring, and affecting her love for education. They were affecting it, just not at all in good ways. In many ways they were infecting it. They appeared to look at her and see just another body in another seat in the classroom. They saw another person they had to police and keep in line until 3:40 p.m. They did not see all of the possibilities. They made her feel unwelcome.

Being deeply versed in the research, the theory, and the data, it was clear that this could impact her connection, her metacognition, her achievement motivation, her self-efficacy, her attributions, and, foundationally, her very love of learning. It was clear that these few teachers in this short time had the power to undo the years of hard work she, her past teachers, and her parents had put into generating and maintaining her love of learning. It was clear that the functioning of the system was beginning to harm this child. It was believed that the research, knowledge, and hard work would keep her safe, but her parents were beginning to feel powerless in protecting her love affair with education and learning.

The fear was that these feelings would devolve into the popular mantras many students repeat at the collegiate level with an owned conviction:

"I'm not good at writing!"
"Math is not my subject!"
"Science is not my thing!"

"I am not good at this!"
"I can't do that!"

These mantras are often coupled with the words "I can't." Words that are akin to self-denigration. The students who make these attributions tend to trace these "beliefs" back to messages they received from teachers along the way, and they came to own them and nurture them through focus, often seasoning them with the word "can't."

In the space of a few months this scholar was disengaging because these few teachers treated her as just another body in the room rather than as a person to connect with, a soul to be seen, a spark to be ignited, or a flame to be maintained. They were beginning to make her feel as though who she was, what she did, and what she liked did not matter. She expressed feeling like she had no power in the situation.

No parent should ever have to mitigate the harmful effect of a teacher on their child's emotional well-being, cognition, or ideology. It was explained to her that it was not the subject that she did not like but the way it was being taught. She craved creativity so the author had to find fun and experiential ways to nurture her love for these subjects.

A parent also should not have to try and persuade their child that the teacher does not (in fact) dislike them. She was clear that she was disliked. Conversations had to be mediated with the teacher to change this perception and to help the student be able to express herself. She had to hear it directly from the teacher, who had to work to reconnect with her.

When they do not feel seen, students receive the clear communication that they are disliked, inconsequential, or unimportant. The Maya Angelou quote at the beginning of this chapter holds glaring truth. Students will always remember how you made them feel whether that was nothing at all, good or bad, safe or unsafe, welcome or unwelcome, able or unable, seen or not seen.

Teachers hold an immense responsibility because they play a vital role in shaping student perceptions of the world and how it works. The unfortunate reality is that although good experiences leave a resounding impact, negative experiences often echo much louder in our brains because they come laced with trauma that tends to play unfiltered on repeat. The cacophony caused by negative experiences can drown out the good that is taking place.

There was a local principal who understood the deep importance of this. He collaborated with the author on teacher diversity trainings for pre- and in-service teachers. He discussed testing potential hires by asking certain questions during the interview that would allow him to tease out responses that revealed how they thought about and valued students from different cultural and socioeconomic backgrounds.

Responses that communicated care, a value for all, and a desire to con-nect were rewarded with an offer of employment coupled with training to strengthen their outlook and effectiveness. Responses that stereotyped or "othered" learners were noted, and those so-called educators were dismissed after conversation regarding their purview. Those educators were not con-sidered to be fit to engage with his students whom he absolutely saw as his (connecting back to the opening Hilliard quote).

Being seen for who we are on our own terms and from the standpoint of how we want to be seen makes us feel indescribably good about ourselves. This distinction is very important. People should be "seen" for who they are projecting themselves to be not for who they are thought to be from media-infused stereotypical views.

This is not just from the superficial visual representation perceived from the physical appearance of others, although this does provide some shallow clues. This is the internal, invisible, and deeper representation of the self that teachers can learn to see through developing a relationship with students and donning culturally sustaining lenses. Being seen makes people feel secure, loved, important, and safe to explore.

This note is important for all teachers. The sad reality is that it does not matter if students have a teacher who is phenotypically similar to them if they have been raised in K–12 and collegiate experiences saturated in mono-culturalism. This creates a veil of misunderstanding, coloring their percep-tions, especially if the students are seen as anonymous others.

Although the assumption may be that these teachers share the same cul-ture and therefore they get it, they too may be unable to see their students if they have not been trained to consider that their contexts have any social, cognitive, or emotional importance. The sad reality is that these teachers can still hold negative views of culturally similar students and transmit harmful messages and biased content. The story of the student shared within this chapter is a prime example.

One thing *all* teachers need to understand is that *every single child* can soar if we simply help them to find, develop, test, and strengthen their wings. Every single child without exception. What they have experienced thus far is not a determinant of how far they can soar. Sometimes these experiences serve to reinforce their wings, making them stronger.

This understanding begins with changing the direction of the view so that the possibility of all students being seen is higher. We begin clearing vision by changing the game. Teacher education has to be changed and enhanced to overhaul and repair the entire system. It is time to retire the old pieces and rebuild, placing students at the center. The old game is obsolete.

~

CHAPTER FIVE

Where Do We Begin?
With Educator Preparation of Course

Our job is not to prepare students for something. Our job is to help students prepare themselves for anything.

—A. J. Juliani

You can teach a student a lesson for a day, but if you teach him to learn by creating curiosity, he will continue the learning process as long as he lives.

—Clay P. Bedford

Introduction

Formal teacher preparation began in the 1820s around the creation of what were called "normal schools" located in Massachusetts and Vermont (Ducharme & Ducharme, 1999). Normal schools were originally created to train teachers based on a European model of teacher education where they learned how to teach specific skills. They were not, however, taught how to think deeply about the skills they were teaching. The knowledge transfer process was procedural in nature.

By the 1940s, most of the normal schools grew into four-year teachers colleges or liberal arts institutions. Through higher education expansion in the 1960s, some of these institutions expanded into state universities. With this expansion, programs moved beyond simple procedure and began to reflect theory-based practice.

The Structure of Teacher Education

Traditional teacher preparation programs consist of a general arts and sciences methods course focus, advanced study in a particular discipline for secondary, teaching methodology, incorporation of learning theories, and field experiences. The Council for the Accreditation of Educator Preparation (CAEP), the new teacher preparation program accrediting body, states that the ultimate goal of teacher preparation is to impact P–12 student learning and development (CAEP Accreditation Standards, 2015). As such, each accredited program must adhere to the following five standards:

1. Content and Pedagogical Knowledge (encompassing the Interstate New Teacher Assessment and Support Consortium [InTASC] standards of learner development, learning differences and environments, content knowledge, application of content, assessment, planning for instruction, instructional strategies professional learning and ethical practice, and leadership and collaboration),
2. Clinical Partnerships and Practice,
3. Candidate Quality, Recruitment, and Selectivity,
4. Program Impact, and
5. Provider Quality Assurance and Continuous Improvement.

The aforementioned standards do not specifically mention diversity or technology because CAEP has set the expectation that these are critical areas that should thread throughout all aspects of educator preparation programs. It is believed that diversity is threaded through each of the standards because the guidelines state that "all students" should be the focus and that "multiple perspectives" must be incorporated into the discussion of content. While this is a positive movement forward, educator preparation programs have only recently been asked to incorporate and adhere to CAEP standards, as it has not yet been officially accepted at the state level.

The current issue is that culture has not been adequately infused in teacher preparation, and there is no specific guide on how to complete this monumental task (CAEP Accreditation Standards, 2015; Lewis & Taylor, 2015; Renner et al., 2004; Villegas & Lucas, 2007). Even with CAEP's attempt to saturate standards with diversity, there are no specific steps delineating what such a program should actually look like. There is also no guidance on how to transform programs that do not infuse culture at an acceptable level.

A number of alternatives to traditional certification have also been created to reach students of diverse backgrounds (that is, Teach for America,

Uncommon Schools, Knowledge Is Power Program, etc.) as the traditional route of educating preservice teachers has been found lacking in the treatment of culture, gender, ability status, and socioeconomic status (Ducharme & Ducharme, 1999; Ladson-Billings, 2008). Although these alternative routes serve target populations and it is possible to find pockets of success, they do not necessarily incorporate cultural considerations, and many of the teachers do not experience the same level of training as certified teachers, a fact that can create its own challenges within those spaces.

Preparing Teachers for CSP

Research has shown that despite the growing population of diverse and English language learner students in American schools, preservice teachers are not adequately prepared to effectively deal with the current reality of diverse classrooms (Castagno & Brayboy, 2008; Hammond, 2015, Hsaio, 2015; Ladson-Billings, 2000, 2008, 2017; Renner et al., 2004; Zhao, Meyers, & Meyers, 2009). The reason for this is twofold. First, the teaching force is not diversifying at the same rate as the student population. Overall, U.S. teachers are overwhelmingly middle class, White, monolingual English speaking, and female.

This brings with it potential cultural, gender, and socioeconomic conflicts. Second, teacher preparation is lacking as it pertains to cultural competence (Hsaio, 2015; Ladson-Billings, 2014; Renner et al., 2004; Villegas & Lucas, 2007). This fact is largely responsible for maintaining the status quo in the education system (Ladson-Billings, 2008).

Most teacher preparation programs, regardless of context, cover content, methods, and basic pedagogical features (that is, content knowledge, pedagogical content knowledge, assessment, professional dispositions, etc.). This gives preservice teachers the knowledge and skills needed to perform the cursory job of teaching. These programs also tend to treat culture as supplemental information to be focused on in one course (if even that) because it is a hot button phrase in the research rather than a priority.

The one course is also not likely covering cultural considerations at any level of depth. As a result, these programs are not integrating culture within overall programmatic pedagogy, and teachers feel overwhelmed by the prospect of "dealing" with culture (Hsaio, 2015; Ladson-Billings, 2008, 2014; Renner et al., 2004; Villegas & Lucas, 2007). It is not uncommon to hear even experienced educators express anxiety over the prospect of incorporating culture or to say that it cannot be done.

HBCUs versus PWIs

Most of the literature on culturally responsive preservice teacher preparation broadly deals with overall preparation. It does not take into account the context within which teachers are prepared and how that might impact whether culture is transmitted or how culture is transmitted. It also is not connecting context with teacher competency, self-efficacy, or outcome expectations.

The research on historically Black colleges and universities (HBCU) and predominantly White institutions (PWI) teacher preparation is varied. Only a few studies focus on culture and diversity, and even fewer include HBCUs and PWIs in the same study (Bakari, 2003; Dilworth, 2012; Sleeter, 2008). More research needs to be conducted in this area because, as CRP reflects, culture is not simply a Black and White issue (Bakari, 2003; Ladson-Billings, 1995b, 2017; Siwatu, 2007).

In terms of the existing literature, there is much support for the need to expand experiences and views for White students. Sleeter (2008) discussed the PWI environment as problematic, stating that "as institutions, predominantly White universities generally reflect the same attitudes and experiences of predominantly White students, and it is as hard to change these universities as it is to change the people in them" (p. 239). It is difficult to change culturally harmful views because they are being nurtured by their education.

In addition to this, Amos (2016) states that it has been continuously documented that White preservice teachers demonstrate resistance to multicultural education, hold negative and racialized dispositions toward diverse students, tend to be naïve about race, and hold stereotypes toward persons of color. These well-documented issues continue to go unaddressed. The researcher also found that Black student teachers at PWIs often encounter racial prejudice within their programs (from professors and fellow students) and do not feel safe reporting these incidents to administration.

Bakari (2003) conducted a study looking at both environments specifically dealing with teaching Black students. He found that HBCU students scored higher in their willingness to teach Black youth than students attending public and private PWIs who expressed more willingness to teach in general compared to Black youth specifically. Students at the private PWI even had specific multicultural programmatic requirements. They found resistance to using culture in the classroom from all participants from both environments.

Williams and Evans-Winters (2005) and Amos (2016) stated that they consistently experience resistance from White preservice teachers in the process of unpacking race, privilege, and systemic inequalities at a PWI, where students at times feel empowered enough to "prey on the instructor" (p. 1008). Many professors do not press too hard because they fear retaliation from students, especially professors who are still on the tenure track. The findings in all three of these studies could be connected to how cultural content is dealt with or not incorporated efficiently.

Lowenstein (2009) states that White teacher candidates are often painted as deficient learners in the realm of culture, calling for more research of teacher preparation programs across the board. The researcher states that although multicultural education is well established, less is known about the actual teaching of preservice multicultural education. It is not clear what these classes actually entail.

Ladson-Billings (2008) states that because these courses are so often supplemental, the information is not put into context and students, particularly White students, are left feeling frustrated and confused not knowing how to process this information. Many students report feeling guilty as their sense of self can become destabilized when confronted with historical inequities. This leads to students feeling defensive, extremely uncomfortable, and resistant in discussing and dealing with culture.

Sleeter (2008) agrees that the preparation of White teachers to educate diverse students needs to be improved substantially. Case studies of PWIs report that diversity and equity are dealt with in a disjointed manner and dependent more upon professor interest in teaching the subject rather than integrated at the program level as excellent teaching practice. The researcher posits that teacher education needs to be powerful enough to counter three forms of ongoing socialization both preservice and in-service White teachers experience:

1. homogenous daily experiences;
2. ongoing homogenous and monoculturally curricular schooling experiences from K–12 to college to teaching; and
3. the banking model of teaching and learning enacted every day in classrooms stemming from the first two experiences.

Irvine and Fenwick (2011) and Dilworth (2012) discuss how HBCUs should be able to establish sound and credible culturally sustaining programs; however, they have not been added to funding streams to support such efforts. They tend to focus on socioeconomic status and placing teachers into high-need schools and urban environments, teaching students who resemble them phenotypically. Hayes and Juarez (2012) discuss White racial domination present in teacher preparation, specifically in PWI spaces.

Fasching-Varner and Seriki (2012) respond to Hayes and Juarez (2012) stating that CRP is actually taught—however, it is not taught effectively. They call for it to be embedded into every single course and professional development. Lastly, Lewis and Taylor (2015) call for research examining the experiences of African American preservice teachers, specifically at HBCUs, and ways to address the complexity of providing diverse experiences for teacher candidates.

Bridging the Gap

Renner et al. (2004) call out teacher preparation programs, asserting that they are shirking their responsibility to assist preservice teachers in developing as global citizens living in a diverse world, which the authors also state is causing serious harm to their future students. Due to this inadequate education, some neophyte teachers also employ the term *culture* as both the "problem and answer" to struggles and frustrations with students with backgrounds differing from their own. This once again identifies these students as others and places them in the deficit perspective.

For example, there is consensus in the literature that teacher expectation is a problem area that must be taken into consideration when discussing the achievement of marginalized students of color (Gay, 2002; Gilbert & Gay, 1989; Hilliard, 1992; Neal et al. 2003; Singh, 2011; Sleeter, 2008; Tucker & Herman, 2002). Hilliard (1992) states that the images teachers hold about children and their potential have a great influence on the range of professional skills utilized with those children. If teachers are not taught to challenge these images during their preservice preparation, it is not likely that this process will happen.

Similarly, Hsaio (2015) points out that teachers' beliefs, attitudes, and knowledge are correlated with student race and ethnicity, as well as the quality of the education they receive. For example, teachers will "teach down" to the estimated level of their students' ability by simplifying, concretizing, fragmenting, and slowing down the pace of instruction to reflect the students' perceived level of ability (Henfield & Washington, 2012; Hilliard, 1992). As a pointed example of this phenomenon, Gilbert and Gay (1989) stated that teachers form opinions about the academic abilities of Black students based on the problems they have with the "procedures of teaching and learning," which are again based on European standards.

These views can be addressed and mitigated through the way preservice teachers are prepared to engage with students from differing backgrounds during their teacher education programs. If this is not done correctly, this sets a self-fulfilling prophecy into motion as some teachers expect African descent students to fail regardless of their actual academic potential. The Curious Case of Ms. M from the introduction is a prime example of this.

She directly communicated to her students that she did not think they could do it. Most teachers will not reflect overt racist beliefs. Many do not realize they may hold harmful views. These stereotypes about performance are not logical, as they do not stem from the student's reality, yet they have a direct effect on the teacher's expectations and treatment of students (Neal et al., 2003; Singh, 2011; Sleeter, 2008).

Many researchers and theorists have discussed the promise of culturally appropriate teacher preparation, which would engender culturally sustaining practice that has the potential to do three things. It would mitigate problematizing marginalized children because teachers would be guided through the process of shedding harmful beliefs. It would improve academic achievement because the focus would be on student learning. It would also benefit youth from all backgrounds (Hammond, 2015; Hsaio, 2015; Irving & Hudley, 2008; Kalyanpur & Harry, 1997; Kea & Utley, 1998; Ladson-Billings, 2000, 2006; Renner et al., 2004; Singh, 2011; Villegas & Lucas, 2002; Zhao, Meyers, & Meyers, 2009).

Villegas and Lucas (2007) and Hayes and Juarez (2012) state that diversity should be infused throughout the curriculum to improve teacher education programs. Another view purports that teacher preparation must include traveling abroad to actually practically interact with other cultures rather than solely engaging in textbook-driven experiences where students are superficially trained to be "culturally competent" through what-if classroom scenarios (Zhao, Meyers, & Meyers, 2009). Yet another view adds service learning projects, such as volunteering in homeless shelters and working in soup kitchens, to the experiential education list (Renner et al., 2004).

Field experiences must be expanded in order to offer students robust experience with students who are culturally different. Programs must move away from the superficial treatment of diversity and culture inherent in teacher education programs across the United States. Abstract ideas are vastly different from tangible firsthand experience. A deeper level of understanding and development takes place when people are able to physically interact with the concept in question (Renner et al., 2004). This involves the letting go of preconceived notions or assumptions in order to be able to authentically experience new phenomena with limited or no bias.

Zhao, Meyers, and Meyers (2009) argue that this will assist preservice teachers in learning to care about and understand the "whole child." Similarly, Dixson and Fasching-Varner (2009) posit that the degree to which teachers acknowledge culture reflects their belief in the "fundamental humanity" of the children they encounter in the classroom. This is a particularly poignant point as the very way in which we socialize teachers to interact with students has the potential to impact, whether for good or bad, their psychological, emotional, and intellectual future functioning.

School is the second point of socialization for children after the home (Aldana & Byrd, 2015; Hughes, 2003). Their school experience holds sway over who they will become. This is pertinent for veteran teachers as well and provides a guidepost for enhancing ongoing teacher professional development. Many individual schools and larger school districts focus on cursory workshops that once again present culture as supplemental and still focus on students from marginalized backgrounds as disadvantaged and deficient (Dixson & Fasching-Varner, 2009; Thompson, 2015a).

These views, even when stemming from good intentions of alerting teachers to cultural difference, are harmful because they perpetuate negative stereotypes and can be overtly or covertly transmitted to students, as discussed earlier. It not only impacts their classroom practice, it also connects to ongoing teacher trainings. Culture could be treated as supplemental in ongoing professional developments because of the way it is not integrated or considered as salient during preservice education.

Teachers unwittingly hold a significant amount of power as it pertains to their influence in the lives of children they encounter (Singh, 2011). Yes, short term they are in charge of transmitting knowledge and to some extent control the grades students receive. Long term the messages teachers send while instructing can affect future achievement, student self-efficacy and academic esteem, student disidentification, as well as negative views of different cultures for White students (Griffin, 2002).

This is why it is vital to address culture and our responses to difference at a deep level during preservice teacher training. In his keynote speech to the National Staff Development Council, Asa Hilliard III had the following to say:

> They [teachers] recognize that outstanding learners can be crippled by the types of exposure they encounter, but they also realize that teaching is a power tool that when used appropriately can awaken the genius in children. (Hilliard, 1997, p. 21)

It is time to revamp teacher education programs and professional developments aimed at diversity to provide teachers with the proper tools and imbue them with the ability to be able to reach all students regardless of background or circumstance. Vital to this toolbox would also be a sovereign, culture-based, and language-infused curriculum free of racism, classism, sexism, and bias (Hanley & Noblit, 2009). However, creating such a curriculum requires educators who are efficacious in acknowledging, unpacking, and applying culture.

Self-Efficacy and Outcome Expectations

General teacher self-efficacy beliefs have been widely studied over the past twenty-nine years (Siwatu, 2011). Little research has been done to investigate preservice or in-service teacher self-efficacy beliefs as they pertain to culturally responsive practice. Traditionally, self-efficacy has been approached from two viewpoints: Rotter's (1966) locus of control or Bandura's (1977) social cognitive theory. This discussion employs Bandura's conceptualization of self-efficacy as the "belief in one's capabilities to organize and execute courses of action required to produce given attainments" (Bandura, 1997, p. 3).

Bandura, as well as subsequent researchers, discussed effective functioning within this particular domain as going beyond the acquisition of knowledge, skills, and competence and extending into the teachers' belief in their ability to apply what they have learned in their teaching practice (Bandura, 1977, 1997; Pajares, 1996; Siwatu, 2007, 2011). Teachers can know the information inside and out; however, if they do not believe they will be successful in applying or transferring that knowledge, then their self-efficacy and performance will be low in that particular domain. This also applies to teaching information they have not themselves mastered.

Bandura (1977) also discussed outcome expectations, defining them as "a person's estimate that a given behavior will lead to certain outcomes" (p. 193) or probable consequences, whether positive or negative, of engaging in the indicated behavior (Pajares, 1996; Pajares, Hartley, & Valiante, 2001; Siwatu, 2007). Chu and Garcia (2014) add that outcome expectations denote a teacher's belief that instruction can have a positive influence regardless of extraneous environmental influences or factors. These definitions combine here to describe the perception of the impact or end result of engaging in pedagogical practice.

Outcome expectations are based on both personal experience and the experience of models. In other words, judgments are made about particular outcomes based on the experience, whether direct or indirect, with the concept in question. As it pertains to this discussion, this would be the outcomes or consequences associated with employing culturally sustaining teaching practices during instruction.

Scholarship in this area is emergent as little research has been conducted to investigate culturally sustaining teacher outcome expectancy beliefs and researchers are recently paying more attention to whether teachers believe that culture-centered practice will lead to positive classroom and student specific outcomes (Chu & Garcia, 2014; Siwatu, 2007). These beliefs are based in the person's reality whether through personal experience with the construct itself or from direct observation of others employing the construct. If preservice teachers are not being taught to employ CSP adequately, they may not feel comfortable with the concept and thus display a lack of confidence in potentially positive outcomes.

According to Bandura (1986), self-efficacy and outcome expectations have a tendency to be correlated, stating that it is difficult to think about the outcome without thinking about what is being done to achieve the result, and how well one is doing it. He stated that the connection between these two constructs produces four patterns: high/high, high/low, low/high, or low/low. He also stated that these patterns produce different affective responses (feelings of self-assurance or self-devaluation) and different behavioral responses (high engagement or withdrawal).

In light of this, one might posit that affect toward the concept in question plays a role in self-efficacy and the outcomes expected from employing it. In line with this, Siwatu (2007) observed a 0.70 correlation between teacher responses on the Culturally Responsive Teacher Self-Efficacy Scale (CRTSE) and the Culturally Responsive Teacher Outcome Expectancy (CRTOE) Scale. In his analysis of item-specific means on the CRTSE, he found that preservice teachers felt more efficacious in their ability to build positive relationships with students and their ability to make them feel like valued members of a classroom community than they did in communicating with English language learners. CRTOE scores were correlated with these findings.

Siwatu (2007) also states that the constructs of self-efficacy and outcome expectations are related but can also be independent. For instance, scores could represent low self-efficacy but high outcome expectations or vice versa. He explains that a novice teacher may have positive outcome expectancy beliefs associated with culturally sustaining practice but doubt her/his ability to effectively implement it, and that correlation between the two constructs may decrease once preservice teachers begin their teaching careers.

Again, all of this is connected to experience and whether preservice teachers are being taught and challenged to interact with culture in meaningful ways. The research clearly shows that this is not happening across the board in any collegiate context. This omission is irresponsible practice, and it is harming American students. This is already widely known. It is also widely ignored. With this, a challenge is issued to the education community to shake the foundation free of stagnation in order to build a new structure.

~

CHAPTER SIX

A Tale of Two Differing Programs

Framing the Study

Research is an expression of faith in the possibility of progress. The drive that leads scholars to study a topic has to include the belief that new things can be discovered, that newer can be better, and that greater depth of understanding is achievable.

—Henry Rosovsky

Research is to see what everybody else has seen, and to think what nobody else has thought.

—Albert Szent-Gyorgyi

Research is formalized curiosity. It is poking and prying with a purpose.

—Zora Neale Hurston

Introduction

So what exactly does teacher preparation for culturally sustaining practice look like right now, real time? Because I truly believe that educator preparation is the key to impactful systemic change, I needed to explore the internal practices in these programs to find solutions and a starting point. I conducted the following mixed method study in order to evaluate how teachers are currently being prepared to deal with the overwhelming culture monster in differing contexts.

This chapter lays out the building of the study (with results included in the next chapter) in order to provide programs with a stepwise framework for evaluating their own practice for programmatic development and enhancement and to provide a snapshot of current preparation practices from the perspective of those who are being prepared to enter the field. It is important to consistently evaluate practice *even* when programs state they have a pointed focus on culture. This study structure assists in deciphering whether transmission is meaningful and provides a guide on how to make adjustments.

Framing the Study

In order to paint this picture, the study measures self-efficacy in delivering responsive lessons, affect toward culturally sustaining practice, as well as whether teachers have been trained to employ certain practices in the process of delivering instruction. If the experience in these two programs reflects research trends of underpreparation in terms of culturally sustaining practice presented in the previous chapter, then it would be expected for the preservice teachers to have lower self-efficacy scores. If CRP is treated as a supplemental concept, then it might be perceived to be as such, leading to less favorable outcome expectations within the domain.

The study seeks to measure whether culturally sustaining practice is being taught in preservice teacher preparation programs, how the information is disseminated to students, and the connection between the level of preparation and preservice teacher self-efficacy and outcome expectations related to the theory. The focus of inquiry includes training received from an HBCU and a PWI in order to explore and compare the level of preparation in both settings. This study also explores whether teachers are employing certain culturally supported constructivist-based practices in the process of delivering instruction.

Mixed methods is a methodology for conducting research that involves collecting, analyzing, and integrating both quantitative and qualitative research. This method was chosen because it is the most adequate and detailed way to address the research questions and shed light on the current state of culturally responsive teacher preparation. This chapter includes the overall study methodology presenting the chosen philosophical paradigm, theoretical framework, contextual information about the schools highlighted in the study, information on participants, procedure, data analysis, instruments (CRTPS, CRTSE, and CRTOE), concluding with delimitations and expectations. The overall design of the study is as follows in figure 6.1.

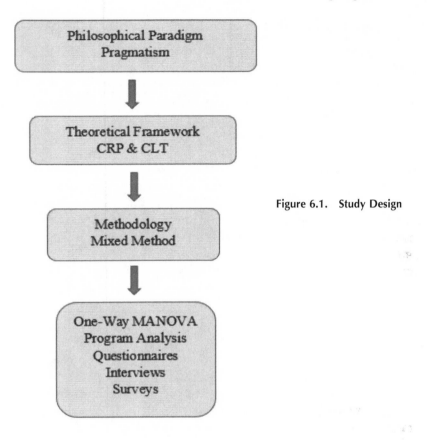

Figure 6.1. Study Design

Philosophical Paradigm

The study is situated within the theoretical paradigm of pragmatism. Here the focus is on finding the truth of meaning that is couched within theories or beliefs in terms of how successful they are in practical application. In other words, it deals with the real-world application of ideas (Cameron, 2011; Creswell, 2012; Feilzer, 2010; Goldkuhl, 2012), taking concepts from the theoretical (this is, what should be happening) into the practical (this is, what is really happening).

According to Creswell and Plano Clark (2011) and Feilzer (2010), pragmatism encompasses features that are associated with both positivism (gaining "socially useful" and applicable knowledge objectively through scientific analysis) and constructivism (the intersection of human ideas, or intelligence, with real-world experiences), without restricting the researcher to choosing between the two worldviews during the research process. It allows for the simultaneous application of both. Just as culturally sustaining practice should be dynamic, it was important to employ a paradigm that reflected that dynamism.

Although pragmatism has been criticized for its eclecticism (Cameron, 2011), one might argue that it is this eclectic nature that provides for flexibility of use. This paradigm allows for the application of a number of research methods and analytical approaches and provides a means of authentication of theoretical principles in practice. Feilzer (2010) argues that it can be applied as a more balanced research approach to inquiry.

This philosophy is ideal for the current study as it employs constructivism as a theoretical framework. The research aim is to measure if CSP is transmitted to preservice teachers through their teacher education programs, the methods of transmission, as well as the depth of that transmission. This connects to Goldkuhl's (2012) explanation of pragmatism as apropos to research that is interested in actually intervening in the world rather than simply observing occurrences and maintaining the status quo.

CSP is a pretty idea in theory. It sounds good and it would be amazing if it were doable. The question is How do teacher preparation programs appropriately and authentically instill this as a practice in future educators avoiding simple lip service to the concept? Many wonder if this can be done given all other deliverables that are required of teachers.

The focus of inquiry in this study is on what works as truth for participants from each institution in terms of application through the research questions. As pragmatism births action from constructive knowledge, this could potentially allow for change and enhancement in the way teachers are actually trained to push through their own discomforts and interface with culture as a foundational and required pedagogical practice. Again, this should just be a part of what it means to be a teacher.

Theoretical Framework

The theoretical framework for the study is based in the frames of culturally responsive pedagogy and constructivism (which is also a feature of pragmatism). Although the theory of culturally responsive pedagogy is currently being updated and transformed through the literature to culturally sustaining pedagogy, this study focused on culturally responsive pedagogy because a viable model of CSP has not yet been created and the instruments reflected responsive practice. Thus, culturally responsive pedagogy here translates to the focus on culture, pathways to optimal student learning, social justice, and social advocacy (Ladson-Billings, 1995b, 2014; Paris, 2012).

CSP would also include Indigenous language revitalization. Stanley and Noblit (2009) state that culturally responsive teaching is simply synonymous with good teaching. This pedagogical theory is both student and culture focused as it begins with what the learner knows, includes students' cultural ways of knowing within the curriculum, and nurtures critical thinking.

Constructivist learning theory (CLT) and culturally responsive pedagogy naturally combine to create a positive, effective, and engaging learning context. The main notion of most constructivist approaches is that students play an active rather than passive role in the learning process (Hamza & Hahn, 2012; Stanley & Noblit, 2009). They are not empty receptacles waiting for information to be dumped on to them. They must participate in order to encode information.

Students employ schema as the pathway to new understanding. CRP enters as that schema is constructed through cultural ways of understanding phenomena. When that schema is intimately meaningful, connecting to that student's worldview and learning style, through information processing the schema is moved into and stored in long-term memory ready to be accessed when needed.

CLT and CRP also connect here as constructivism purports that because ontology, or the nature of being and existence, is beyond human understanding, no culturally based viewpoint is more accurate or better than another (Hamza & Hahn, 2012). No culture is superior to any other because what matters is what is relevant to a particular learner so all viewpoints hold equal value (Kea, Campbell-Whatley, & Richards, 2006; Ministry of Education, 2013; Villegas & Lucas, 2007). This combined framework promotes and supports multiple views creating global thinkers who learn to think critically about and engage with the world around them.

Additionally, Villegas and Lucas (2002) purport that culturally responsive teachers have three roles that are grounded in constructivism:

1. Teachers within this context "understand how learners construct knowledge and are capable of promoting knowledge construction.
2. Teachers know about the lives of their students.
3. Teachers design instruction that builds on what their students already know while stretching them beyond the familiar." (p. 20)

Constructivism, similar to CSP, contends that all students can learn and it is the teacher's role to create the bridge between prior knowledge and new information in order to support learning for each child (Kea, Campbell-Whatley, & Richards, 2006). These theories interconnect in a dynamic interflowing way. Interestingly aspects of each theory reinforces aspects of the other.

Methodological Approach

In order to decide on the mixed method design and sampling scheme, it was important to first analyze the mixed method goal, research objectives, and research purpose (Creswell & Plano Clark, 2011; Onwuegbuzie & Collins, 2007). The overall goal of this study was to add to the knowledge base on culturally responsive pedagogy, to understand this complex phenomenon (or how and to what extent it is transmitted to preservice teachers in different environments), and to potentially affect institutional and social change (to take action). The research objectives are exploration and explanation leading to implementation.

The purpose in employing mixed methods for this particular study was to examine how data overlaps and converges in the findings to provide as accurate a picture as possible. Next, the four factors of type of interaction, priority, timing, and mixing were considered in order to settle on the specific approach and design. This study represents independent interaction as there are separate research questions for the qualitative and quantitative strands, data is collected concurrently, and data is merged during interpretation.

The two strands are equally prioritized and presented concurrently to provide context to the responses. Due to these factors, a convergent parallel mixed methods design was selected and employed in order to measure culturally responsive teacher preparation. Here qualitative and quantitative methods are equally prioritized; data is collected simultaneously in a single phase, analyzed separately, and then merged in the interpretation of the results (Creswell, 2014; Onwuegbuzie & Collins, 2007). (See figure 6.2.)

Convergent designs also fit well when the overall philosophical paradigm of the study is pragmatism (Creswell & Plano Clark, 2011). Employing this design creates a holistic view of the research questions by merging them with fully fleshed out stories to shed light on potentially congruent findings. There are consequences to having different sample sizes when merging results. To guard against this, an equal number of participants were recruited from each institution. There are also potential challenges in merging two different types of data.

In this study, a one-way multivariate analysis of variance (MANOVA) is conducted to test the theory of culturally responsive pedagogy through administration of three inventories. Respondents were given the Culturally Responsive Teacher Preparation Scale (CRTPS), the Culturally Respon-

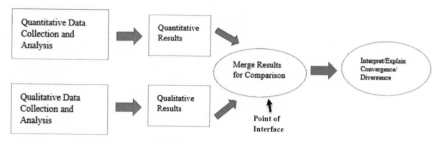

Figure 6.2. Methodological Approach

sive Teaching Self-Efficacy Scale (CRTSE), and the Culturally Responsive Teaching Outcome Expectancy Scale (CRTOE). Through these inventories, the MANOVA analyzes what is being taught in the way of CRP.

The focus is on testing whether attending a teacher preparation program at an HBCU or a PWI influences how participants have been prepared. Their level of preparation is expected to be reflected in their self-efficacy in delivering responsive lessons, affect toward cultural responsivity, and outcome expectations for employing CRP. The study also measures whether teachers have been trained to employ certain practices in the process of delivering instruction.

In the qualitative portion, the program analysis, qualitative questionnaires, and faculty interviews explore whether CRP is infused throughout programmatic offerings or whether it is treated as supplemental. These answers also provide context to quantitative scores, giving insight into personal feelings respondents may have about CRP in general. This is expected to shed light on how they have been prepared to apply it in their practice through their educational program.

The reason for collecting both quantitative and qualitative data is to account for weaknesses found in either design and to gain a full understanding of the research questions and CRP preparation in general by obtaining different, however complementary, data. Mixed methodology here provides more of a complete picture of teacher preparation, allowing for the analysis of whether the results converge or diverge (Creswell & Plano Clark, 2011; Onwuegbuzie & Collins, 2007). For instance, the program analysis specifically provides an evaluation tool for cultural-based preparation and at the same time provides context to overall scores on the measures.

Mean scores reveal whether the teachers are prepared to be culturally responsive, how they feel about CRP, if they are student centered, if they employ contextual teaching, as well as if they are able to tap into student prior knowledge in order to build understanding. Through a synthesis of the work of Hollins (1993), Gay (2002), and Siwatu (2006) identifying competencies for teaching diverse populations, Hsaio (2015) provides a comprehensive definition for culturally responsive teachers:

> Responsive teachers are those who challenge their biases, deliver culturally responsive instruction, identify students' needs, communicate with students and parents, design and implement curricula creating a caring and supporting setting, and enrich students' diverse cultures through instruction.

The research questions were split into quantitative, qualitative, and mixed method in order to provide a map as to which part of the design addresses each question. Research questions were as follows:

Quantitative MANOVA-Based Research Question:

Is there a statistically significant difference between mean CRTPS scores, mean CRTSE scores, and mean CRTOE scores for teachers who attended either the PWI or the HBCU?

- H_o: There is no statistically significant difference on mean CRTPS scores, mean CRTSE scores, and mean CRTOE scores between teachers who attended the HBCU or the PWI, or $\mu1 = \mu_2 = \mu_3 = \mu_k$.
- H_a: There is a statistically significant difference on mean CRTPS scores, mean CRTSE scores, and mean CRTOE scores between teachers who attended the HBCU or the PWI, or $\mu1 \neq \mu_2 \neq \mu_3 \neq \mu_k$.

Qualitative Research Questions:

- Is culturally responsive pedagogy infused throughout the preservice teacher program or is it treated as supplemental?
- How do preservice teachers feel about culturally responsive pedagogy?
- What do preservice teachers think about the culturally responsive preparation they received?

Mixed Method Research Question:

- To what extent do the quantitative and qualitative results converge or diverge?

Quantitative Data Analysis

In order to examine the quantitative research question, a one-way MANOVA was conducted to determine whether there is a statistically significant difference on mean CRTPS, CRTSE, and CRTOE scores by institution. This measures whether scores differed from HBCU to PWI. The dependent variables (DVs) in this analysis are mean CRTPS scores, mean CRTSE scores, and mean CRTOE scores, and the independent variable (IV) is type of institution with two levels (HBCU or PWI) (see table 6.1).

The research question is testing the main effect of the IV on the DVs. Global mean scores as well as item-specific responses were analyzed. Siwatu (2007) states that global scores provide insight into the factors that influence self-efficacy and outcome expectations, and item-specific means on the CRTSE and CRTOE "may prove to be useful to teacher educators and program administrators who are interested in fine-tuning programmatic efforts to prepare culturally responsive teachers" (p. 1097).

Table 6.1.

Type	HBCU	PWI	
N	13	13	26

The MANOVA assumptions of multivariate normality, homogeneity of the covariance matrices, the independence of observations, absence of multivariate outliers, linearity, and the absence of multicollinearity were assessed prior to running the analysis. Multivariate normality assumes that all of the DVs are normally distributed (bell shaped), which should be satisfied as the sample size is more than ten times the number of groups (two), satisfying the central limit theorem. The sample size of twenty-six meets the assumption of sufficient sample size by level of the independent variable (two levels).

The Shapiro-Wilk test is employed to verify normality. Homogeneity of the covariance of matrices assumes that variance shared between any two variables is equal across all levels of the independent variable. The homogeneity assumption is tested using Box's M. Independence of observations assumes that a participant's scores on the dependent measures are not influenced by or related to scores of any other participant in the condition or level. This is satisfied by the design of the study as participant scores are independent and have no influence or bearing on one another.

The absence of multivariate outliers checks for data that might impact the variance observed in the analysis. This would be represented by scores that skew the results. It is assessed via evaluation of Mahalonobis distances (the distance between two points in a multivariate space) among the respondents through multiple linear regression (explains the relationship between one continuous DV and multiple IVs) and checked against critical chi square values to determine significance.

Linearity assumes that dependent variables are linearly related across each level of the independent variable. When plotted on a graph, the data should be so close together that you can draw a straight line through it determining the direction of the data. This assumption is assessed by conducting and evaluating scatterplot matrices.

Lastly, the absence of multicollinearity checks for high correlation between variables that could impact variance scores. Collinearity is checked by conducting correlations among the dependent variables through regression analysis. The CRTSE and CRTOE are expected to be highly correlated (Bandura, 1986; Siwatu, 2007) as self-efficacy and outcome expectation are connected. A high score on one measure would reflect a high score on the other.

Employing MANOVA rather than simply running a series of individual ANOVAs is advantageous for a number of reasons. First, MANOVA takes into account possible intercorrelations among the dependent variables that would have bearing on the findings if unchecked. Individual ANOVAs may not produce a significant main effect on the DV because it does not consider those connections, but in combination through MANOVA they might. This might suggest that the variables are more meaningful grouped together than they are separate.

It is of value to the current study because the DVs (self-efficacy and outcome expectation) are actually related. Second, if the normality assumption is met, MANOVA is more powerful than separate tests. On the other side, MANOVA is limited because it is a more complex test and results may be ambiguous. The multiple DVs could have effects on each other, which could be confused with effects of the IV. Follow-up analyses are employed and reported in order to address this concern and ensure that the results are what they seem to be.

Qualitative Data Analysis

The study employed program analysis, surveys, questionnaires, and interviews in order to investigate cultural considerations in teacher preparation. The program analysis was conducted via evaluation materials from each program (HBCU and PWI). The conceptual framework, policies, program handbooks, course offerings and descriptions, and demographic information (faculty makeup/areas of expertise, student population, demographics of the surrounding area) were appraised.

Each aspect of the program was evaluated via the Program Culture/Diversity Evaluation (PCDE) Rubric. The rubric was developed and adapted from the New England Resource Center for Higher Education (NERCHE) Self-Assessment Rubric for the Institutionalization of Diversity, Equity, and Inclusion in higher education (Lewis et al., 2016). The original rubric was used as a college-wide measure. The PCDE rubric was reworked to be employed at the individual program level.

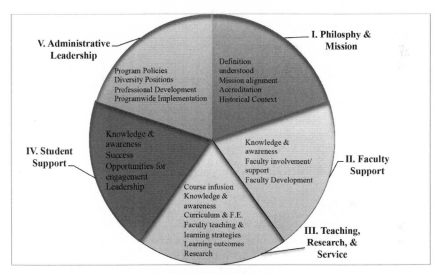

Figure 6.3. Program Evaluation Rubric Five Dimensions

The NERCHE rubric was used as a guide in the creation of the program evaluation rubric to gauge the level of integration of cultural considerations throughout the teacher preparation programs. The portion dealing with program frameworks and paperwork provides a guide of what each program "says" it is doing in regard to culture. The faculty interviews and teacher qualitative responses inform what is actually taking place in the programs as opposed to simply going by what the paperwork states. The rubric consists of five dimensions measured through specific program components and artifacts (see figure 6.3 and appendices).

Dimension one, Philosophy and Mission, evaluates the historical context of culture and diversity in relation to the program, established definitions and operationalization of the construct, accreditation considerations, and mission alignment. Dimension two, Faculty Support, focuses on the degree of faculty ownership of culture and diversity in terms of development opportunities, knowledge and awareness, as well as involvement in and support of diversity activities. The third dimension, Teaching, Research, and Service, searches for evidence of diversity in courses, the overall program curriculum, importance to student learning outcomes, and faculty foci or research.

The fourth dimension, Student Support, is very much tied to the third dimension. This component searches for evidence of student knowledge, awareness, outcomes, leadership, and opportunities for engagement in diversity activities. Lastly, dimension five, Administrative Leadership and Programmatic Support, analyzes program policies, diversity-specific teaching positions, professional development opportunities, and program-wide implementation of culture and diversity. These program components were each evaluated and sorted into one of four stages of development (no evidence, emerging, developing, and transforming) to gauge the level of program infusion.

Qualitative questionnaire responses and interviews were examined through the application of thematic analysis (see table 6.2). This form of analysis requires paying attention to detail allowing for data descriptions to develop in opulent detail. According to Braun and Clarke (2006), this type of analysis consists of six stages, which in essence include viewing the data several times, identifying patterns or emerging themes, and reorganizing data to reflect those patterns.

Qualitative responses and faculty interviews were coded for patterns and themes, which allowed for the creation of a visual comparative checklist. Thematic analysis is advantageous because it is not tied to any one theoretical framework in the same ways other methods might be, which permits application with a variety of theories across epistemologies, so this method fits with the paradigm of pragmatism (which is also flexible) and the frames of CRP and constructivism. Braun and Clarke (2006) state that it works to both "reflect reality, and to unpick or unravel the surface of 'reality'" (p. 83).

The focus is on providing appropriate answers to the research question(s). This allows for expansion past individual experience to look at what is really taking place in each program, staying true to pragmatism. The interpretation of themes is supported by the data, so it allows for categories and themes to emerge from the data rather than making data fit prescribed themes.

Braun and Clarke (2006) and Guest (2012) also discuss disadvantages to employing thematic analysis. First, the amount of flexibility in the analysis can make it difficult to zero in on exactly what parts of the data should be focused on, which can also lead to missing important aspects of the data if

Table 6.2. Six Phases of Thematic Analysis

Phase	Process	Result
Phase 1	Read and reread data to become familiar with it, paying specific attention to and noting any visible patterns.	Preliminary "starting" codes. Detailed notes about code meanings. Source of the code.
Phase 2	Generate initial codes (documenting where and how patterns occur). Data reduction (collapsing data into labels in order to create categories for a more efficient analysis). Data complication (making inferences about what the codes mean). Provide info about how and why codes were combined, what questions are being asked, and how codes are related.	Comprehensive codes related to how the data answers research questions.
Phase 3	Combine codes into themes that accurately reflect the data. Describe *exactly* what the themes mean (how codes were interpreted and combined to form themes), even if the theme does not seem to "fit." Describe what is missing from the analysis.	List of possible themes for further analysis.
Phase 4	How do themes support both the data and the theoretical perspective? If analysis seems incomplete, go back and find what is missing. Answers to research questions and data-driven questions need to be well supported by the data.	Coherent recognition of how themes tell an accurate story about the data.
Phase 5	Define what each theme is, which aspects of data are being captured, and what is interesting about the themes. Describe each theme within a few sentences.	Comprehensive analysis of what the themes contribute to understanding the data.
Phase 6	Decide which themes make meaningful contributions to understanding what is going on within the data. Conduct member checking (check the data to ensure descriptions are accurate representations of the data).	Final themes identified and description of the results.

not careful. Second, the discovery and verification of codes and themes can mesh together if the researcher is not vigilant.

The six-phase process safeguards against this by making sure verification is checked against the actual data. Lastly, reliability is of concern due to the number of interpretations that can arise from the themes. These disadvantages can be controlled through the coding process.

Because the end goal of the process is to gauge actual impact rather than perceived impact, qualitative responses were analyzed through the emergent strategy of double blind coding. This allows raters to follow the constructive nature of the data itself and prevent any possible bias as the codes emerge directly from the data and raters are not aware of the codes assigned by one another. Four coders were engaged in the process to gauge the coefficient of agreement and to garner interrater reliability, teasing out the actual consistent themes in experiential responses.

Employing more than one rater safeguards against nuances in the data being glossed over during analysis. It also ensures that interpretations of themes are not driven by one singular thought process that is attempting to find proof of something rather than seeing a phenomenon for what it is. This reduces opportunities for researcher bias to surface and hijack the evaluation process.

Participants

The following study consists of twenty-six teachers and four faculty members from two liberal arts institutions located in Georgia that offer teacher education preparation programs, thirteen teachers and two faculty members from each institution. The institutions consist of one predominantly White institution (PWI) and one historically Black college (HBCU). The sampling scheme was nonrandom (or nonprobabilistic). Purposeful sampling was utilized, representing criterion (they fit the desired categories) and convenience (Onwuegbuzie & Collins, 2007).

The research goal called for two specific settings, a PWI and an HBCU. The two settings represented in the study were then selected due to convenience to the researcher. Teacher respondents were mostly female (twenty-four) with a small number of males (two) and were Black and White. Faculty respondents were all female, three Black and one White.

MANOVA analyses typically call for larger sample sizes in order to generate sufficient power. Onwuegbuzie and Collins (2007) state that it is appropriate at times to utilize small samples in quantitative analyses. The sample size for teachers was selected after considering accurate representation for the populations of interest, the appropriate sample size for running MANOVA (Onwuegbuzie & Collins, 2007), and running an a priori power analysis calculation using G*power to determine the power needed for the study (see figure 6.4).

Table 6.3. G*Power Output

Input Parameters:	Output Parameters:
Effect size = 0.8	Noncentrality parameter λ = 20.800
A err prob = 0.05	Critical F = 3.049
Power (1 – β err prob) = 0.95	Numerator df = 3.000
Number of groups = 2	Denominator df = 22.000
Response variables = 3	Total sample size needed = 26
	Actual power = 0.952
	Pillai V = 0.444

The analysis was for F tests and MANOVA global effects. Effect sizes are interpreted as either small (0.2), medium (0.5), or large (0.8). If the power is less than 0.8, then the sample size needs to be increased in order to reduce the chances of making a type II error (rejecting a true hypothesis). Power calculations for this study were as shown in table 6.3.

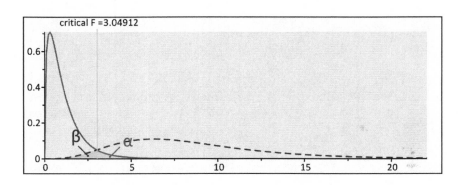

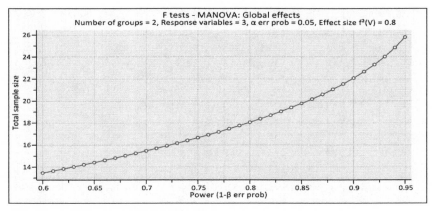

Figure 6.4. G*Power Output Graph

The estimated actual power of 0.952 shows the data has the potential to mitigate the crisis of representation that can arise with studies having samples too small to accurately distinguish statistically significant findings (Onwuegbuzie & Collins, 2007).

Procedures

Forty alumni teachers were recruited from two Georgia teacher education programs in order to maintain respondent anonymity and ensure that enough data was collected. Twenty-six responses were included in the analysis in line with G*power requirements for sample size, as well as due to the number of full responses received. Data was analyzed, coded, and reported in terms of programmatic offerings related to diversity and CRP (program conceptual framework, program policies and handbooks, course descriptions and offerings, faculty research and expertise, field experiences, professional development opportunities).

Two faculty members from each program were interviewed in order to provide descriptions of the institutions and determine whether CRP is infused within the teacher education curriculum or whether it is treated as supplemental. A qualitative questionnaire, the CRTPS, the CRTSE, and the CRTOE were administered in a single packet online via the Qualtrics online survey creation and distribution platform. Teachers gave self-reports regarding their affect toward and self-efficacy in cultural responsivity as well as their perceptions of CRP preparation in their teacher education program.

The surveys and questionnaire took approximately thirty to forty-five minutes to complete. The CRTPS consists of eighteen items, the CRTSE consists of forty-one items, the CRTOE consists of twenty-six items, and the qualitative questionnaire consists of ten open-ended questions, and an additional four contextual culture-driven questions to gauge how teachers think about culture. Participants were notified that their information would be kept confidential, and to ensure that their responses were not directly linked to them, they were asked to enter an alias in the name slot of the questionnaire.

Research Contexts

The population of the study consists of four faculty members (two from each institution) and twenty-six teachers (thirteen from each college) from two institutions located within the same state in the southern area of the United States. Institution 1 is a historically Black liberal arts college located within an urban area. The school is ranked 72 out of 239 among first-tier liberal arts institutions and 69 in High School Counselor Rankings.

Institution 2 is a predominantly White liberal arts college located within a rural area. The school is ranked 174 out of 239 among liberal arts institutions and 80 on the High School Counselor Rankings. These schools were chosen specifically for the desired demographics and researcher transportation accessibility. Indicators used to ascertain the academic quality of these institutions include

- graduation and first-year student retention rates (22.5%),
- undergraduate academic reputation (22.5%),
- assessment by administrators at peer institutions, faculty resources (20%),
- student selectivity (12.5%),
- financial resources (10%),
- alumni giving (5%),
- graduation rate performance (7.5%),
- and high school counselor ratings. (Morse, Brooks, & Mason, 2016)

Instruments

The CRTPS is a multidimensional, eighteen-item inventory employing a six-point Likert-type scale ranging from unprepared to fully prepared, measuring teacher preparedness to execute the practices associated with culturally responsive teaching (Hsaio, 2015). Factor analysis of the original thirty-two-item scale revealed three measurable categories or factors across eighteen items: (1) curriculum and instruction (items 1–8), (2) relationship and expectation establishment (items 9–14), and (3) group belonging formation (items 15–18). The CRTPS was found to be reliable with Cronbach's alpha for the whole inventory 0.95, and 0.91, 0.91, and 0.88 for the three factors respectively. Hsaio (2015) also reports that the CRTPS tests fairly in relation to implementation across gender and race.

Developed by Siwatu (2007), the creation of the forty-one-item CRTSE and the twenty-six-item CRTOE was guided by the theoretical and empirical research on teacher self-efficacy beliefs and outcome expectations and culturally responsive teacher preparation. Grounded in Bandura's (1977) construction of self-efficacy, the CRTSE was designed to reflect a wide range of culturally responsive teaching practices, and the CRTOE reflects respondent beliefs about outcomes associated with those practices. Future work will entail the creation of a scale that can measure culturally sustaining practice, incorporating Indigenous language revitalization as a vital construct.

Both scales utilize a 0 to 100 response format where 0 is entirely uncertain, 50 is not too certain, and 100 is completely certain. Pajares, Hartley, and Valiante (2001) found that this type of scale was psychometrically stronger than the traditional Likert-type scale when measuring a construct such as self-efficacy, stating that greater discrimination (or offering expanded choices) provides for more accurate prediction. Both scales were found to be reliable with the Cronbach's alpha of 0.96 on the CRTSE and 0.95 on the CRTOE.

Delimitations

Delimitations are defined as those characteristics within the researcher's control that limit the scope and define the boundaries of the study (Simon, 2011). Pragmatism was chosen as the guiding philosophy because of the flexibility it allows in applying quantitative and qualitative methods as well as the focus of understanding the reality of the program through the integration of multiple methods to provide a more detailed picture of what is happening in teacher preparation in regard to culture. The scope of the study was narrowed to two schools from four to lighten the qualitative load.

The schools were chosen in terms of travel accessibility. The study was also originally going to employ a factorial MANOVA; however, the number of IVs was reduced from three to one because it was determined that the research questions could be addressed better with the one IV on institution type (HBCU vs. PWI). This was changed to a one-way MANOVA to fit the new parameters.

Expectations

The following convergent parallel mixed method study will shed light on culturally responsive teacher preparation including affect toward and efficacy/outcomes expected in employing the construct. In line with the current research, CRP was expected to be treated as supplemental in both teacher preparation programs rather than completely integrated into the overall curriculum. This was expected to be reflected in the program analyses, as well as through faculty interviews and student qualitative responses. Also in line with research trends, the HBCU was expected to have slightly higher global and item-specific scores than PWI teachers because of the institutional focus on culture.

CHAPTER SEVEN

~

A Tale of Two
Differing Programs Continued

The Numbers

In fact, quantitative findings of any material and energy changes preserve their full context only through their being seen and understood as parts of a natural order.

—Walter Rudolf Hess

If you do not know how to ask the right question, you discover nothing.

—W. Edward Deming

Introduction

Just to reiterate, the purpose of the study presented in the previous chapter was to explore culturally responsive teacher preparation in differing environments. The goal was to provide a picture of how preservice educators are currently being prepared to engage with the culture of their future students within instruction. The results of this study provide a starting point for an overhaul of the education system from the foundation up.

CRP (and now CSP) preparation has been identified as a means to obviate the marginalization of students of color, to connect them to the education system in meaningful ways, and to engage them at deeper levels. It has also been identified as a curricular asset for students of all backgrounds engendering positive cognitive and academic outcomes. Teacher self-efficacy and outcome expectations, as they pertain to culturally responsive pedagogy, are also assessed gauging how likely teachers are to apply theory to practice and engage in responsive classroom behaviors.

This chapter includes the overall mixed method study results, beginning with a presentation of the descriptive characteristics of participants. Remember that in convergent parallel mixed method design, data is collected simultaneously, analyzed and reported separately, then merged in the results. The study results are presented here in the same order with quantitative analyses, qualitative analyses, and a mixed method discussion of how data merged during parallel analysis.

As part of the purpose is also to provide a guide for program evaluation to initiate change, all steps are described in detail. The quantitative section includes research questions and hypotheses, MANOVA assumptions, MANOVA analyses, and post hoc tests. The culturally responsive teacher preparation scale (CRTPS), the culturally responsive teacher self-efficacy scale (CRTSE), and the culturally responsive teacher outcome expectancy scale (CRTOE) were employed as the dependent variables of the analysis, with institution type (historically Black college versus predominantly White institution) as the independent variable.

The qualitative section includes program evaluation results and answers to qualitative research questions via a report of corresponding participant responses from interviews and questionnaires from the HBCU and PWI teacher preparation programs. The program evaluation was conducted using the Program Culture/Diversity Evaluation (PCDE) Rubric. This assessment tool was adapted for the program level and employed to evaluate various aspects of each teacher preparation program to garner the degree to which the consideration of culture is infused within overall program functioning, requirements, and outcomes.

Presentation of Descriptive Characteristics of Respondents

Study participants were originally expected to represent U.S. national trends in the teaching profession with PWI trained teachers being mostly White and female and HBCU students being mostly female and 100 percent Black. There were no expectations for the cultural backgrounds of participating faculty members as this could be variable. The original research request to teachers received forty responses; however, only twenty-six were complete and able to be added into the analyses. In line with the G*power analysis parameters (see chapter 6), data included thirteen participants per cell (twenty-six total), giving the findings sufficient power.

Respondents also reflected the national trends. Of the responses from the PWI, all thirteen were White females with eleven trained for early childhood education and two for secondary. HBCU teacher responses included thirteen full responses. All thirteen were Black (eleven women, two men), ten of whom were in early childhood education and three in secondary. Four total faculty responded to the email inquiry for participation. Faculty from the PWI included two women professors (one Black and one White). HBCU faculty were both Black women professors. (See table 7.1.)

Table 7.1. Participant Demographics

	HBCU		PWI	
Designation	Faculty	Teacher	Faculty	Teacher
N	2	13	2	13
Ethnicity:				
Black	1	13	2	0
White	1	0	0	13
Sex:				
Female	2	11	2	13
Male	0	2	0	0
Program				
Type:	—	10	—	11
ECE Sec	—	3	—	2

Quantitative Research Question and Associated Hypotheses

The quantitative research question and corresponding hypotheses for the study were as follows:

- Is there a statistically significant difference between mean scores on the Culturally Responsive Teacher Preparation Scale (CRTPS), mean scores on the Culturally Responsive Teacher Self Efficacy Scale (CRTSE), and mean scores on the Culturally Responsive Teacher Outcome Expectancy Scale (CRTOE) for teachers who attended either the HBCU or the PWI?
- H_0: There is no statistically significant difference on mean CRTPS scores, mean CRTSE scores, and mean CRTOE scores between teachers who attended the HBCU or the PWI, or $\mu 1 = \mu 2 = \mu 3 = \mu k$.
- H_a: There is a statistically significant difference on mean CRTPS scores, mean CRTSE scores, and mean CRTOE scores between teachers who attended the HBCU or the PWI, or $\mu 1 \neq \mu 2 \neq \mu 3 \neq \mu k$.

In terms of the quantitative analysis, it was expected that the null hypothesis would be rejected with HBCU-trained teachers receiving slightly higher scores on the CRTPS, CRTSE, and CRTOE. This expectation is in line with the research that discusses monocultural practices centered in Whiteness across institution type (Hayes & Juarez, 2012)—specifically, PWI students as having more discomfort in discussing and unpacking culture (Sleeter, 2008; Bakari, 2003; Amos, 2016), and HBCU students being slightly more comfortable given the fact that these institutions deal directly with culture and historical inequities in higher education attainment (Bakari, 2003; Lewis & Taylor, 2015).

Research also discussed HBCU teacher preparation dealing more with lower socioeconomic areas than necessarily having wider and more diverse understandings of culture (Irvine & Fenwick, 2011; Dilworth, 2012). Because of this, HBCU student teachers are typically tracked into field experience placements with students who are phenotypically similar to them. Each of these patterns was expected to be reflected in the findings.

Checking Assumptions of MANOVA

Before running the quantitative analysis, it was important to ensure that the data did not violate the characteristic assumptions of MANOVA by checking the assumption of multivariate normality, the absence of multivariate outliers, linearity, absence of multicollinearity, and the equality of covariance matrices. Multivariate normality was assessed via the Shapiro Wilk test, which evaluates whether the CRTPS, CRTSE, and CRTOE responses are statistically significantly different from a normal distribution (see figure 7.1).

With the CRTPS, the null hypothesis was retained, as scores were found to be normally distributed presenting an alpha of 0.429. A value greater than the limit set of $\alpha = 0.05$ assumes normality. Less than or equal to $\alpha = 0.05$ assumes a nonnormal distribution. The null hypothesis was rejected for the CRTSE and CRTOE, both with an alpha of 0.000. This was expected given the 0 to 100 response format of these two scales, which allows for greater variability between scores. This expectation is further explained by the remaining assumptions.

Checking for multivariate outliers reveals extreme cases (individual means) that could potentially impact the analysis of the data. This was checked by running a flipped multiple linear regression with CRTPS, CRTSE, and CRTOE scores entered as the independent variables (instead of DVs) by institution type as the dependent variable (instead of the IV). Mahalanobis distances among all participants were then analyzed.

Mahalanobis distance measures the distance between a given point P (student individual mean scores) and a distribution D (the center point of the overall mean). This score demonstrates how many standard deviations student scores are away from the mean of D. This reveals if any of the individual scores are numerically different from the rest, which could change how the data is perceived.

Mahalanobis distances alone revealed one possible outlier in the data. Before this outlier is confirmed, the assumption must be substantiated with further analysis by comparing it to the critical chi square distribution limits (χ^2 = 16.27, p = 0.001), with degrees of freedom equaling the number of dependent variables in the analysis (df = 3). The chi square is employed to compare two categorical variables in order to determine the degree to which they are related.

One outlier was identified in the dataset with a critical chi square of (χ^2 = 18.327, P_MD = 0.00038). This case presents as a multivariate outlier (a combination of unusual scores) but is not necessarily a univariate outlier (an extreme value on one variable). Whereas this outlier value would normally be removed before analysis as not to alter the results, it was retained here because of the nature and function of the scales employed in the study. A closer look at the data revealed that the CRTPS responses were aligned, as it is a typical six-point Likert-type scale.

The CRTSE and the CRTOE, however, allow students to choose their level of self-efficacy in performing tasks related to cultural responsivity and their degree of certainty that given responsive behaviors would lead to positive outcomes on a scale of 0 to 100. Because the scale is so spread out, an outlier is not necessarily a predictor that something has gone awry with the data but rather an indication of individual and subjective efficacy and outcome expectation. As Pajares, Hartley, and Valiente (2001) point out that expanded choices of a 0 to 100 scale lead to greater predictability, it was also understood that they could lead to outliers in the data for these two scales.

Linearity of the data assumes that the dependent variables of the study (the inventories) are all linearly related to one another for each group (HBCU and PWI). The data should appear along a straight line when represented by a graph. This was evaluated via the scatterplot matrices represented in figure 7.2.

The scatterplot shows a linear relationship for all plots. It also shows that a positive relationship exists between the CRTPS and the CRTSE (p = 0.001, r = 0.613) as well as between the CRTPS and the CRTOE (p = 0.021, r = 0.451). Reflecting Bandura (1986) and the findings of Siwatu (2007),

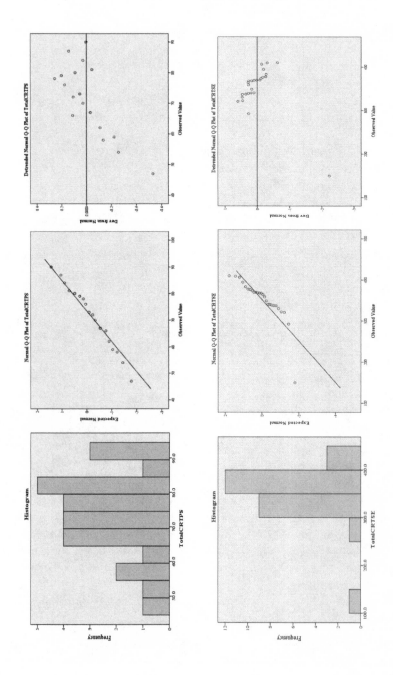

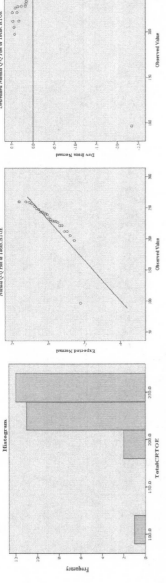

Figure 7.1. Shapiro Wilks Normality of the DVs

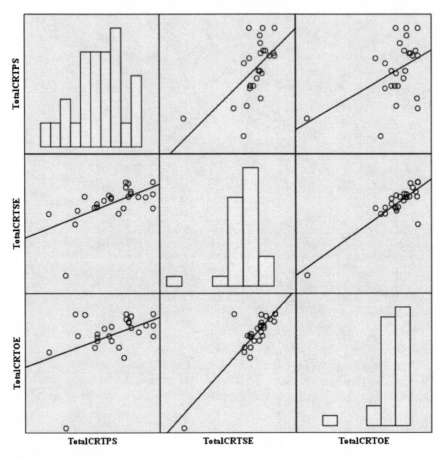

Figure 7.2. Linearity of DVs

the CRTSE and CRTOE have a strong positive relationship (p = 0.000, r = 0.866), meaning as self-efficacy goes up, so too do outcome expectations.

Bandura (1986) stated that the constructs of self-efficacy and outcome expectations have a tendency to be related. Siwatu (2007) reported a correlation of 0.70 between the two scales; however, the researcher acknowledged that though correlated, self-efficacy and outcome expectancy can also be independent depending on specific teacher beliefs. The multivariate outlier case is also represented in the histograms for CRTSE and CRTOE as the point located away from the line. The scatterplot matrices indicate that the assumption of linearity is met through the data.

Table 7.2. Collinearity Statistics

Model	Tol.	VIF	Model	Tol.	VIF	Model	Tol.	VIF
TotalCRTSE	0.249	4.012	TotalCRTOE	0.797	1.255	TotalCRTPS	0.624	1.601
TotalCRTOE	0.249	4.012	TotalCRTPS	0.797	1.255	TotalCRTSE	0.624	1.601
DV:			DV:			DV:		
TotalCRTPS			TotalCRTSE			TotalCRTOE		

The next assumption of MANOVA is multicollinearity, or high correlation between two variables that influence divergence in data. Absence of multicollinearity was checked by conducting correlations among the CRTPS, CRTSE, and CRTOE responses through regression analysis. Regression analysis estimates relationships between the DVs and the IVs, or rather should there be an observed difference in scores based on which school context teachers have been trained in. Corresponding output is represented in table 7.2.

Popular cutoff values for multicollinearity are a tolerance score of 0.1 with a variance inflation factor (VIF) of 10 or a tolerance score of 0.2 with VIF of 5. A potential issue arose with the CRTPS showing moderate correlation with the CRTSE and CRTOE (Tolerance = 0.249, VIF = 4.012). Neither score surpassed the 0.2 and 5 threshold.

According to Obrien (2007), VIF thresholds should be considered within context of other variables. The researcher also stated that smaller sample sizes can inflate regression coefficients. This coupled with the known correlation between self-efficacy and outcome expectancies explains the values.

The assumption of multicollinearity does not only check whether there is a relationship. It also checks to make sure there is enough of a relationship between the DVs. According to Field (2017), MANOVA works best when DVs are only moderately correlated, as is the case with the current data. Thus, the moderate correlation is actually desirable for MANOVA and does not warrant any correction.

The final assumption, equality of covariance matrices, measures equal variance across samples (in both HBCU and PWI responses). MANOVA tends to be robust to this assumption when sample sizes are equal (Field, 2017), so the expectation is that this assumption is met given the equal sample sizes in the study. Homogeneity of covariance is checked via the Box's M test, which sets a strict significance level of $\alpha = 0.001$.

Box's M for the current data reveals a statistically significant result of $\alpha = 0.031$. Although this number is significant, it is not below the 0.001 limit, which would present a problem. The findings fail to reject the null hypothesis, meaning the data meets the assumption of equal covariance matrices.

Multivariate Analysis of Variance

Once the assumptions were examined, the quantitative hypothesis was tested via a one-way MANOVA conducted in SPSS (Statistical Package for the Social Sciences). The independent variable was institution type with two levels, HBCU and PWI. The three dependent variables were CRTPS scores, CRTSE scores, and CRTOE scores. Results are presented in terms of descriptive statistics, Box's M test of equality of covariance matrices, multivariate tests, Levene's test of equality of error variances, between-subject effects, and multivariate test results.

Table 7.3. MANOVA Descriptive Statistics

	Institution Type	Mean	Std. Deviation	N
TotalCRTPS	HBCU	80.462	7.2757	13
	PWI	66.462	10.5957	13
	Total	73.462	11.4131	26
TotalCRTSE	HBCU	374.308	25.8396	13
	PWI	329.762	59.4943	13
	Total	352.035	50.3529	26
TotalCRTOE	HBCU	240.369	16.5247	13
	PWI	221.092	41.5605	13
	Total	230.731	32.5081	26

An initial look at descriptive statistics (table 7.3) shows that PWI had a lower mean than HBCU for each DV, thus the null hypothesis is rejected as HBCU teachers did in fact receive higher scores. This is in line with the findings of Hayes and Juarez (2012). Results show that HBCU-trained teachers feel better prepared to employ culturally responsive pedagogy, have a higher level of belief in their ability to carry out tasks associated with culturally responsive teaching, and also have more positive outcome expectations than their PWI trained counterparts (Sleeter, 2008; Bakari, 2003; Amos, 2016).

This was in line with the expectation that HBCU-trained teachers would have higher scores than PWI-trained teachers. As discussed by Bandura (1986), the HBCU showed a higher level of self-efficacy and higher outcome expectations. Both groups scored highest in outcome expectations across the three measures. This showed a low/high self-efficacy to outcome expectation pattern for the PWI (Bandura, 1986). This was unexpected for the PWI as the assumption was that expectations would mirror the level of comfort (Chu & Garcia, 2014; Siwatu, 2007) reflecting a low/low pattern.

Box's M test shows a value of F = 2.321 and α = 0.031. Because Box's M sets a strict alpha level of 0.001, the test fails to reject the null hypothesis that observed covariance as equal across groups, meaning there was some variance observed in the scores. Pillai's Trace was selected as the multivariate analysis to test overall significance because of the Shapiro Wilk's results indicating multivariate normality (α = 0.429).

Pillai's Trace presents a statistically significant difference (α = 0.008) across institution type on a linear combination of the CRTPS, CRTSE, and the CRTOE. Further analysis reveals where the difference exists in order to definitively answer the quantitative hypothesis. The partial eta squared (η^2 = 0.407) does reveal that 40.7 percent of the variance in the DVs can be explained by institution type, HBCU versus PWI.

This is considered a medium effect size representing that the DVs differ by more than 0.4 deviations. Levene's test was conducted to identify exactly where the differences exist between the DVs. The test reveals no significant differences between error variances in the DVs (CRTPS α = 0.238, CRTSE α = 0.240, CRTOE α = 0.202). The test fails to reject the null hypothesis.

A deeper look at the between subject effects initially indicate a statistically significant difference between institution type for the CRTPS (α = 0.001) and CRTSE (α = 0.021). This would reject the null hypothesis for both the CRTPS and CRTSE and fail to reject the null hypothesis for the CRTOE (α = 0.133). To control for familywise error (making a false discovery that is not there) when conducting multiple comparisons, Bonferonni's correction was applied to the critical alpha value for significance.

The original critical alpha level of 0.05 was divided by the number of DVs (3) providing a new critical alpha of α = 0.017 to garner if the variance truly exists. Applying this limit retains significance for the CRTPS. The CRTSE is no longer significant, so the null hypothesis is rejected for level of preparation (which was found to be significant) but retained for self-efficacy and outcome expectations (not significant).

To put it plainly, there should be an observed difference in level of preparation received depending on which school teachers attended. Also, the levels of self-efficacy and outcome expectation are not necessarily tied to the depth of preparation. This could represent a disconnect between an understanding of the concept and what it can produce.

Subscale Findings

CRTPS subscale descriptive statistics (table 7.4) matched the overall scale results. Scores for curriculum and instruction (CI), relationship expectation establishment (REE), and group belonging formation (GBF) also showed slightly lower means for PWI respondents on each of the scales. These results show that HBCU trained teachers feel more comfortable tweaking curriculum and altering instruction to be more culturally responsive, feel better prepared to establish optimal relationships with their diverse students, as well as establish a classroom community optimal for development in school and the global community.

Interestingly, the scores were highest for both groups (HBCU and PWI) in relation to GBF and lowest for both groups on CI. This indicates teachers feeling more confidence in their preparation for forming relationships with students than actually implementing a responsive curriculum. This is where a discrepancy is observed between higher self-efficacy and outcome expectation scores and the level of depth of understanding of the construct. Responses showed that teachers were not necessarily comfortable with CRP but they self-reported feeling they could do it. They may not have a full understanding of what the IT is.

Table 7.4. CRTPS Subscale Descriptive Statistics

	Institution Type	Mean	Std. Deviation	N
CRTPS_CI	HBCU	34.7692	4.43760	13
	PWI	28.3077	3.66025	13
	Total	31.5385	5.17092	26
CRTPS_REE	HBCU	26.6923	2.62630	13
	PWI	22.1538	4.65199	13
	Total	24.4231	4.36507	26
CRTPS_GBF	HBCU	19.0000	1.58114	13
	PWI	16.0000	3.46410	13
	Total	17.5000	3.04959	26

Post Hoc Test

Post hoc tests are employed in order to recheck study findings. They provide a second look to see if the results are really representative of the data—whether the researcher is really seeing what they think they are seeing. Discriminant function analysis (DFA) was conducted as a post hoc test for the overall MANOVA to measure whether there is actually an *observed* difference between scores on the CRTPS, CRTSE, and CRTOE.

Here DFA helps determine the probability of whether respondents were trained at the HBCU or the PWI based solely on looking at the scores. The assumptions for discriminant function analysis are the same as those for MANOVA, as it is simply MANOVA in reverse. Therefore all assumptions have already been addressed, checked, and reported.

The first step is to assess eigenvalues, which determine the direction and strength of a relationship between variables. Eigenvalues of the DFA were observed as 0.685 with an acceptable canonical correlation (identification of latent variables) of 0.638. A value of one is considered a perfect correlation. The canonical correlation squared is equal to the eta-squared value of 0.407 in the original analysis, again representing that 40.7 percent of the variance in the DVs is explained by institution type. Larger eigenvalues explain stronger function. The function here is somewhat strong and found to be at an acceptable level for the parameters of the study.

The null hypothesis that there is no significant discriminating power in test variables was tested using Wilk's Lambda (λ). The DFA returned a λ = 0.593 with an α = 0.008. A lower value for Wilk's Lambda is desirable as it indicates low within group variability, meaning that the scores for a certain group (that is, PWI-trained teachers) should be similar. With power set at the 0.05 level, the null hypothesis is rejected as data shows there may be significant discriminating power present in the DVs (or whether teachers were trained at the HBCU or the PWI).

The next step of the analysis is to check for the relative importance of each independent variable. (See table 7.5.) Standardized Canonical discriminant function coefficients show that the CRTPS (0.851) has the highest discriminating power, followed by the CRTSE (0.510), and the CRTOE (−0.354). Respondent scores on the CRTPS were the best predictor of either HBCU or PWI training in culturally responsive practice. As expected, self-efficacy and outcome expectations were more subjective given the range in scores from 0 to 100 (Pajares, Hartley, & Valiante, 2001).

Table 7.5.   Ranking of Variables

Variable Rankings	Predictor Variable
1	TotalCRTPS
2	TotalCRTSE
3	TotalCRTOE

Classification Results of the discriminant function analysis predicted which respondents were trained at either the HBCU or the PWI teacher preparation program based on their total scale scores. The results show that overall, 80.8 percent of the data was correctly classified. Of the participants, twelve were correctly identified as HBCU (92.3 percent) with only one wrongly identified ($^{12}/_{13}$), and nine were correctly classified as PWI (69.2 percent), with four incorrectly sorted ($^{9}/_{13}$).

The discriminant function indicates good predictive capacity in estimating whether a respondent was trained at the HBCU or PWI based on their perceived level of preparedness, level of self-efficacy, and outcome expectations. In other words, teachers trained at this PWI are more likely to have low scores on the CRTPS, the CRTSE, and the CRTOE, indicating less cultural focus and preparation and lower self-efficacy and outcome expectations. Teachers trained at the HBCU are more likely to have higher scores on these measures.

The quantitative data reflected some of what was expected based on the research. The next chapter presents the qualitative data that was collected simultaneously. The qualitative portion provides context to the numbers represented in this chapter. The goal is to assess whether this data paints a similar picture to the quantitative findings and provides deeper explanation to phenomenon.

~

CHAPTER EIGHT

A Tale of Two
Differing Programs Continued

The Narratives

We think we listen, but very rarely do we listen with real understanding, true empathy. Yet listening, of this very special kind, is one of the most potent forces for change that I know.

—Carl Rogers

The trick is to produce intelligent, disciplined work on the very edge of the abyss.

—David Silverman

Introduction

Quantitative and qualitative data were collected simultaneously to support the convergent parallel mixed method design of the study. The qualitative analysis was employed in order to provide context to scores on the quantitative measures and evaluate whether the quantitative and qualitative data converge to provide a more accurate picture of culturally responsive teacher preparation in the two programs. The qualitative portion also represents steps educator preparation programs can take to evaluate their own level of functioning to make adjustments where needed.

It was initially expected that culture would be treated as a supplemental aspect of the program, that it would be mentioned and vaguely referred to in program documents, however not included or integrated into actual practices in any meaningful way. Participant responses are merged to answer the research questions and also to represent a dependable and accurate reporting of the data (Baxter & Jack, 2008).

Qualitative Research Questions and Expectations

The program analysis, faculty interviews, and a teacher questionnaire were designed to answer the following questions:

1. Is culturally responsive pedagogy infused throughout the preservice teacher program or is it treated as supplemental?
2. How do preservice teachers feel about culturally responsive pedagogy?
3. What do preservice teachers think about the culturally responsive preparation they received?

Question 1 is addressed through the overall program analysis, faculty interviews questions 1 through 10, and teacher questionnaire numbers 1, 3, 4, and 9. Question 2 is addressed via teacher qualitative questionnaire numbers 2, 6, and 8, focusing on teacher feelings about CRP, and feelings of resistance and comfort in dealing with culture. Question 3 is evaluated via teacher questionnaire responses 5, 7, 9, and 10 focusing on cultural experiences, level of depth of cultural discussions, resistance in the program, and recommendations to enhance culturally responsive preparation of teachers at their respective alma maters.

Teacher participants were also presented with contextual CRP-based questions to provide insight into their responsive thinking in diverse classroom scenarios. It is important to note that these questions simply provide a picture of thought process and whether teachers are making connections between the construct of CRP and classroom situations. Their answers do not, however, tell whether teachers would apply the techniques they are suggesting in their actual practice.

Program Evaluation

The program analysis was conducted through the PCDE Rubric adapted from the NERCHE Rubric (Lewis et al., 2016). The program diversity rubric contains five dimensions; each including a set of measurable components that characterize the dimension. The dimensions represent the key programmatic areas examining the inclusion of culture and diversity in the teacher education program as represented through artifacts.

For each component of the rubric, four stages of development have been established: no evidence, emerging, developing, and transforming (figure 8.1). Progression through the stages would suggest that a program is moving closer to fully infusing culture, diversity, and culturally responsive practice. Indicators for the components include student outcome data, course offerings and descriptions, field experience/placement information, program mission/vision/conceptual framework, faculty expertise and research, and anecdotal evidence.

Figure 8.1.   Program Evaluation Rubric Stages of Development

When a program is at stage 1, there is no evidence of this particular component found within any of the indicators. At stage 2 the program is beginning to recognize culture and diversity as a programmatic priority. Stage 3 recognizes that the program is focused on ensuring the development of its programmatic and individual capacity to recognize and sustain culture and diversity within the component. If stage 4 is indicated, the program has fully integrated culture and diversity into the fabric of the program considering this particular component and continues to assess its efforts to ensure progress and sustainability.

Once at the transforming stage, the program has reached its initial goals for integrating culture and diversity into preservice teacher preparation. The key word here is initial. They have not arrived at an endpoint. In line with Paris (2012), Ladson-Billings (2017), and Paris and Alim (2014), in order to be transformative, the program must recognize the ever-changing nature of education and development and continue to assess its progress and the sustainability of CRP or CSP. Stage 4 is not the destination, it is the beginning.

The initial aim for this study was to engage in double blind coding using two raters. Four raters, all educators, were actually employed in the process to protect against the disadvantages of thematic analysis: missing important data, meshing discovery and verification of codes, and questionable reliability (Braun & Clark, 2006). Three of the raters were not made aware of the research surrounding the topic of culturally responsive teacher preparation specifically highlighted in the current study.

They worked solely from the data presented to move through the six-step process of thematic analysis with each stack of data (HBCU faculty responses, HBCU teacher responses, PWI faculty responses, and PWI teacher responses). They each worked independently with one stack at a time. All raters essentially viewed/read through the data several times, summarized the findings from each element of each stack, then reread the data and identified patterns or emerging codes.

Coders then reorganized the data to reflect those patterns and lastly identified themes and subthemes across the responses. The researcher then took responses from the other three raters, merged the four responses, and created an initial grid of themes and subthemes representing the four groups of findings. Overlapping themes and subthemes were identified and merged in the results (Baxter & Jack, 2008). The researcher then met with the coders to garner agreement before producing the final coding schemes for faculty, teachers, and the anecdotal questions; see tables 8.1, 8.2, and 8.3, respectively.

Raters were not acquainted, nor were they aware of codes or themes assigned by fellow raters. As a first step in the process, the raters evaluated program information and offerings to determine a mean rating for each institution (the HBCU and the PWI). All four raters were employed in this phase of the process for continuity in terms of coding. The raters worked independently to score each institution separately on cultural infusion across the five dimensions, which also provided mean scores for each element of the dimensions.

Interrater reliability was found to be good (given there were four different raters) according to the Altman Kappa Benchmark Scale or substantial according to the Landis and Koch-Kappa Benchmark Scale for both institutions. There was 73 percent agreement for the HBCU program analysis, and 63 percent agreement for the PWI program analysis (Altman, 1991; Gwet, 2014; Landis & Koch, 1977). The discrepancies found here for the PWI were between giving a score of 1 (no evidence), or 2 (emerging) on the four-point scale; however, the scores were always close.

Table 8.1.   Percentage Interrater Reliability

Dimension	HBCU Agreement	PWI Agreement
Philosophy/Mission	0.56	0.69
Faculty Support	0.67	0.83
Teaching Research/Service	0.54	0.68
Student Support	0.56	0.75
Admin. Leadership	0.81	0.63
Total Agreement	0.63	0.73

Philosophy and Mission

The first dimension evaluated was Philosophy and Mission. An important aspect of infusing CSP across teacher preparation programs is the establishment of a shared and consistent definition of culture and diversity that provides both meaning to and focus for infusion and optimal transformation. The more narrowly defined the construct is, the more intrinsic it will be to program functioning; and the reverse is also true.

Components included definitions of culture and diversity (HBCU = 3.13, PWI = 2.25), mission alignment (HBCU = 3.75, PWI = 2), accreditation (HBCU = 3.63, PWI = 2.25), and historical context (HBCU = 4, PWI = 2). The overall mean score for Philosophy and Mission for the HBCU and the PWI was 3.63, developing and moving toward transformation, and 2.19, emerging, respectively. The teacher preparation program at the HBCU appears to have an operationalized definition of cultural diversity and has moved toward a deeper level of application and engagement across levels.

Culture and diversity appear to be primary concerns for the program. They are integrated into different courses, the mission, program policies, and the conceptual framework of the program. Programmatic information gives the impression that the HBCU is engaged in the process of building a more integrated program.

In terms of the PWI, the teacher preparation program was found to be currently at the emerging level. The mission and conceptual framework vaguely mention creating pathways to "success for all" but do not expressly mention culture and diversity and do not offer one operationalized definition of what this means to the program or to student practice.

Culture remains on the periphery, mentioned tangentially in the overall mission of the college (that is, stating that the college will create diverse experiences but not explaining what this looks like). It is not expressly stated in any of the program documents. Culture and diversity are acknowledged but do not appear to be defined or widely understood in this rural and largely monocultural environment. This observation connects back to the findings of Hayes and Juarez (2012).

Faculty Support for Involvement in Culture and Diversity

The second dimension measured the degree to which faculty view culture and diversity as essential to the program curriculum, as well as faculty participation in program efforts related to diversity. The three components of this dimension were faculty knowledge and awareness (HBCU = 4, PWI = 2.75), faculty involvement and support (HBCU = 4, PWI = 3), and faculty development (HBCU = 3.4, PWI = 3). The overall mean score for faculty support and involvement indicator was 3.84 for the HBCU (developing and moving toward transformation), and 2.92 for the PWI (emerging and moving toward developing).

The HBCU faculty in general appears to be knowledgeable about and aware of the importance of culture in teacher preparation. A number of these faculty members participate in transmitting, discussing, and advocating for culture both program-wide and in their individual classes and research. There is a lot of support for student development in this area but a need for more dedicated funding to support faculty capacity to engage in culture-specific training and work outside of national conferences that may include a diversity strand in programming that faculty may or may not attend. There is a need for specific developmental training (Hsaio, 2015).

The PWI has an adequate number of faculty who appear to be aware of what culture and diversity are. A smaller number, however, see them as essential to teacher preparation, advocate for their infusion in the program, or incorporate them into their research or course foci. There is some funding and support for student development—however, not necessarily for faculty-specific development.

Teaching, Research, and Service Supporting Culture and Diversity
Particularly of interest to this third dimension was the degree to which faculty are involved in the implementation and advancement of epistemologies, pedagogies, research, scholarship, and service related to culture and diversity. The seven components included in this dimension were course infusion (HBCU = 3.88, PWI = 2), knowledge and awareness in relation to the program (HBCU = 3.63, PWI = 2.63), curriculum (HBCU = 4, PWI = 2.75), field experiences (HBCU = 3.63, PWI = 2.75), faculty teaching and learning strategies (HBCU = 3.38, PWI = 2.88), student learning outcomes (HBCU = 3.75, PWI = 2.38), and research (HBCU = 3.63, PWI = 2). Overall scores on this dimension were 3.7 for the HBCU (developing and moving toward transformation) and 2.48 for the PWI (emerging).

The HBCU has a few courses focused specifically on culture and diversity and have woven them into the frame of all courses in terms of objectives, a diversity statement, and student learning outcomes. Students appear to be provided the opportunity to engage with (to experience) different aspects of culture regularly. A number of faculty incorporate multiple ways of knowing, employ inclusive practices, appear to be aware of how their beliefs impact classroom learning, and conduct culturally specific research (that is, culturally responsive pedagogy, race and class, exceptionalities, African American history, American Sign Language, and spirituality/religion).

The curriculum and programmatic change efforts indicate a strong value for and commitment to diversity whereby development is guided by learning from new and diverse influences. Documents indicate that field experiences are coordinated with attention to providing multilevel diverse experiences (urban/suburban, socioeconomic status, culture, exceptionalities, and differentiation). There is an indication that students need to receive more support in being culturally sustaining in their practice while in the field in terms of understanding how to practically implement CRP.

The PWI offers a small number of courses focused specifically on culture and diversity. The depth of focus is questionable. Culture and diversity are also integrated into course objectives and student learning outcomes in only a few classes. A small number of faculty appear to recognize how their ways of knowing impact their teaching style and classroom learning and integrate inclusive practices responding to the backgrounds and experiences of their students.

Few faculty conduct research showing a commitment to diversity (that is, exceptionalities). Although the curriculum and program development efforts acknowledge a value for culture and diversity, it focuses on some areas, ignoring others, and is not consistent across program documents or practices. Program information states that field experiences are diverse; however, CRP is not emphasized in the field and the rural makeup of the surrounding community presents a challenge for providing true diversity of experience.

Student Support for and Involvement in Culture and Diversity
Dimension four focused on measuring the extent to which students are provided opportunities to engage with culture in the classroom, the program, as well as participate in leadership activities creating opportunities to experience culture. The four components evaluated were student knowledge and awareness of culture (HBCU = 3.75, PWI = 2.5), student success indicators related to culture (HBCU = 3.13, PWI = 2.38), student opportunities for engagement (HBCU = 3.75, PWI = 2.5), and student leadership opportunities (HBCU = 3.5, PWI = 2.75) for culture and diversity. Overall scores on the student support dimension were 3.53 for the HBCU (developing and moving toward transformation) and 2.53 for the PWI (emerging moving toward developing).

The HBCU is settled in the center of developing and transforming. Students appear to understand the definition and essential nature of culture in relationship to their education and future work. The program appears to link engagement with culture and diversity to student success through offerings and requirements. A number of opportunities exist to enhance student experiential learning and leadership in this area through faculty engagement and collaboration with community members.

The PWI is centered between emerging and developing on this dimension. While some students know that culture and diversity are essential to their education and future work, some still do not acknowledge it in this capacity. Opportunities exist to enhance student learning, but it is not meaningfully integrated into the program or connected to successful outcomes. Opportunities also exist for students to take on leadership roles advancing diversity in the program (that is, participating in the planning of diversity summits), but the depth at which culture is discussed and processed during the summit as well as in classes is a concern that begs the question of whether they are actually advancing diversity (Hsaio, 2015; Ladson-Billings, 2008; Renner et al., 2004).

Administrative Leadership and Programmatic Support for Culture and Diversity

It is important that program leadership demonstrates a commitment to support cultural infusion efforts and ensures resources for and accountability toward those efforts. The four components evaluated were program policies (HBCU = 3.5, PWI = 1.88), diversity positions within the program (HBCU = 3.5, PWI = 1.38), professional development opportunities (HBCU = 3.5, PWI = 2), and program-wide implementation (HBCU = 3.5, PWI = 1.75). Overall scores on the administrative leadership/programmatic support dimension were 3.5 for the HBCU (developing) and 1.75 for the PWI (slightly emerging).

The HBCU again rests solidly in the center of developing and transforming. Program policies and guiding documents recognize culture and diversity as essential aspects of teacher preparation. Professional development opportunities exist for faculty to meet the needs of diverse students, and there is a faculty member who works specifically to advance engagement. Pointed diversity training for faculty would enhance this dimension and bring the program to the transforming level. The formal academic program integrates culture and diversity into multiple levels of the program (courses, field experiences, collaborations with external institutions, travel, etc.).

The PWI is moving toward emerging in this area. The program appears to recognize the importance of culture and diversity; however, they have not been anchored within policies, program documents, or courses in a meaningful way. Although there are faculty who promote and advocate for them, there is not a faculty member who works specifically to enhance culture, and there is also little diversity within the professor pool. Program-wide infusion may be at the beginning stages.

Faculty Interviews and Teacher Questionnaire

Two faculty members from each institution were recruited to participate in interviews and provide information about what is taking place in their respective teacher preparation programs. Responses provided context to program evaluation findings as well as teacher quantitative and qualitative data. Table 8.2 provides the coding scheme for their responses to the ten interview questions and tables 8.3 and 8.4 depict the themes that emerged from the teacher questionnaire data. Answers to the three qualitative research questions are provided via a blend of program evaluation results, faculty interviews, and teacher qualitative response sets to provide a unified picture of program functioning.

Infused or Supplemental

Research question 1 asks whether culture is infused throughout the teacher preparation program or whether it is treated as supplemental. This was important given that both programs claim to focus on diversity. This question was answered via the program analysis (program mission, conceptual framework, program policies, course offerings and descriptions, rubrics, field experience information) presented earlier, as well as through a synthesis of faculty interview responses 1 to 10, and teacher questionnaire numbers 1 (personal definitions of CRP), 3 (diversity of field experiences), and 4 (CRP class integration).

As a starting point to investigating cultural infusion in preparation, the faculty and students were asked to provide their personal definition of culturally responsive pedagogy. CRP has been defined for this study as challenging personal biases, delivering culturally responsive instruction, identifying students' needs, communicating with students and parents, designing and implementing curricula creating a caring and supporting educational setting, and enriching students' diverse cultures (Hsaio, 2015). The goal was to see how much of this operationalized definition showed up in their responses.

Personal Definitions of CRP. HBCU faculty responses reflected the study definition identifying CRP as meeting cultural needs through the following four themes: being *asset oriented*, offering *diverse perspectives*, and going *beyond awareness* of difference to being *open-minded* by welcoming and accepting difference, and incorporating experiences and action.

Table 8.2. Faculty Response Coding Themes and Subthemes

Dimension	HBCU Themes	HBCU Subthemes	PWI Themes	PWI Subthemes
CRP Defined	Open Minded	*Welcome/Accept* *Disposition*	Cultural Integration	*Lived Experience* *Connections* *Incorporating* *Information*
	Asset Oriented	*Student Lived Experience* *Student Centered*	Asset Oriented	*Student Centered* *Student Lived Experience*
	Diverse Perspectives	*Meet Cultural Needs* *Culturally All Encompassing*	Diverse Perspective	*Cultural Realities* *Course Information*
	Beyond Awareness	*Direct Action* *Field Experience/Travel*		
CRP Importance	Necessary	*Successful Process* *Successful Outcome*	Vital	*Unbiased* *Awareness of All*
	Empowerment	*Reach Potential* *Thrive as Educator*	Meaning Making	*Connections* *See Self in Content*
FE Diversity	Levels of Diversity	*Ethnicities* *Socioeconomic Status* *Type of School*	Lack of Diversity	*Rural* *Monocultural*
	Travel	*N/A*		
Class Integration	Integrated	*Multiple Experiences* *Field Placement*	Intentionality	*Intent for All Classes* *On the Record*
	Travel	*Study Abroad*	Requirements	*Program Requirement*
Student Resistance	No Resistance	*Open Minded* *Interested*	Resistance	*Defensiveness* *No Deep Exploration* *Fear of Persecution*

Category	Sub-code	Detail	Further Detail
Personal Resistance	No Resistance		
	Lack of Exposure		
		Fear	Student Retaliation
			Alienating Students
			Being Labeled
		Challenging Beliefs	Different Views
			Responsivity
Other Faculty Resistance	No Resistance	HBCU = Comfort	
		Resistance	Fear
			Lack of Respect
Culture in Instruction	Every Class	Importance	
		Topic Connection	
	Culture Encompassing	N/A	
	Microaggressions		Implicit Bias
			Ignorance
		Complicity	No Accountability
			Confrontation
		Weekly	Current Events
		Modeling	N/A
Depth of Diversity	Varying Depth	Depends on Content	
		Program Embedded	
	Impactful Experience	Processing	
		Experiential	
		Shallow	Depends on Professor
			Need Reflection
		Not Impactful	Intangible
			Making Efforts
Enhancing CRP Prep	Global FE	Teach in a Different Country	
	What of CRP	Teach Explicitly	
		Diverse Faculty	Exposure
		Family Engagement	More Interaction
		Why of CRP	Importance
			Impact

Being culturally responsive means that you are going beyond an awareness level that there are different cultures. There is an action that follows. You have a perspective that you are able to use, in being able to effectively engage, relate to, and teach those of diverse backgrounds.

Two of the HBCU teachers provided surface level one-line definitions (that is, "How you can actually provide instruction on culturally responsive education"). The majority of the responses revealed three overarching themes: *incorporating culture*, *intentional planning*, and *bridging gaps*. Teachers provided multiple examples of CRP ultimately entailing an awareness and understanding of student backgrounds employed in intentional planning to recognize and incorporate multiple perspectives leading to teaching without bias, differentiation, meaningful learning, bridging gaps, and nurturing global awareness.

Culturally responsive pedagogy means teachers are intentional when planning so that their lessons reflect every individual in that classroom in some way, shape, or form. Being culturally aware of the students in your classroom helps to bridge gaps and open new opportunities for dialogue that can contribute to the classroom.

These teachers appear to have a good understanding of many of the elements of CRP as it pertains to the operationalized definition. Further inquiry gauges whether their preparation also focused on implementation.

The PWI faculty response themes for CRP definitions were *asset oriented*, *cultural integration*, and *diverse perspective*. Both discussed CRP as being asset oriented, but one meant internal to students and the other external to students in terms of diverse perspectives.

To be culturally responsive is to connect learning inside the classroom to the realities of people's lives outside the classroom. Culture informs everything we do. To be culturally responsive is to be asset oriented. In this way, the background knowledge and experiences every student brings to the table have value and contribute to more complex and relevant understandings of the world.

Faculty 1 connected it to what students bring to the course. Faculty 2 discussed the incorporation of diverse research. Neither discussed challenging biases as a road to being responsive, which has been identified as an important part of CRP preparation (Hsaio, 2015). PWI-trained teacher response themes were *asset oriented* and *incorporating culture*. Respondents provided a range of surface-level explanations (that is, "It is teaching that is centered on the student and their culture and background knowledge") to only a couple of rich definitions of CRP. For example, one teacher from the PWI provided the following definition:

> Culturally responsive pedagogy refers to an educator being explicit when planning and teaching to be aware and inclusive to the varying cultures of the students in your classroom. Oftentimes, teaching with CRP can help your students develop a stronger mastery to the content because they are able to make deeper and more personal connections. CRP also promotes this sense of respect to cultures in the classroom, teachers, and students. All of this with a hope to make a deeper connection with students and move towards achievement.

Overall, CRP was identified across PWI teacher responses as being an asset-oriented, student-directed and -centered process including all cultures, explicit planning, welcoming of difference, and personal connections leading to mastery of content, deeper personal connections, and achievement. Only one student spoke in terms of addressing biases in the process. This suggests that a couple of the students demonstrate an understanding of what CRP entails beyond surface-level thinking, and some may be a little more comfortable with the construct than others, perhaps indicating that it is discussed to some degree in the program but not necessarily in a consistent manner given the variety in responses.

The Importance of CRP. As an additional indication of program infusion, faculty were asked whether they felt CRP was important to successful classroom outcomes. Themes emerging from these responses were *necessary* and *empowerment* for HBCU faculty and *vital* and *meaning making* for PWI faculty. All faculty across both institutions discussed CRP as being vital to their programs. HBCU faculty spoke in terms of empowerment, successful processes, and outcomes for students reflecting a program-wide focus.

> Cultural Responsivity is of the utmost importance in classroom instruction. If a teacher does not embrace a child's cultural background and learning style, the child's learning can become stifled and the child may not reach his or her potential.

PWI faculty on the other hand discussed its importance a little more abstractly in terms of connecting to their students and meaning making on a person-to-person level with connections to a global community. For example, Faculty 2 from the PWI had the following to say:

> From my perspective, cultural responsivity is vital to an unbiased education. If the asset orientation that seeks to make connections is missing, the outcomes

are compromised. To reject cultural responsivity is to diminish opportunities for meaning making.

Faculty from the PWI are using key terms that can be found in the literature on CRP; however, it does not seem to connect to the way in which teachers will go on to work with and impact students with diverse backgrounds (Ladson-Billings, 2014; Renner et al., 2004; Villegas & Lucas, 2007).

Field Experience Diversity. When asked about the nature of field experiences at their respective institutions, both HBCU faculty stated that field experiences were in multiple diverse environments even though the college has a singular cultural focus. Themes for the diversity of field experience were *different levels of diversity* and *travel.* They identified specific placements in urban and suburban, high and low socioeconomic status, single gender, coed, public, charter, and private school environments as well as candidates completing placements specific to working with students with exceptionalities.

Faculty 1 also mentioned travel as a form of experience, reporting that the program has created a study abroad trip for education students that allows candidates to visit and experience schools in another country (Zhao, Meyers, & Meyers, 2009). Teacher responses mirrored faculty reports with the themes of *different levels of diversity* and *exceptionalities* arising from the data. Teachers identified placements as including cultural diversity, linguistic diversity, low socioeconomic status, high socioeconomic status, single gender, urban, suburban, private, and exceptionalities. One teacher respondent stated, "The diversity in the field experiences was extremely beneficial towards locating my first placement of teaching" postgraduation.

The PWI faculty theme for diversity of experience was *lack of diversity.* Both professors discussed the rural and monocultural nature of the surrounding area in their responses. Faculty 2 noted the lack of diversity in the community as well as on campus as "a challenge to providing true diversity of experience for pre-service teachers." Teacher questionnaire responses echoed this concern with the themes of *lack of diversity* and *exceptionalities* arising.

Teachers reported field experiences as rural and largely monocultural (with a sprinkling of Latinx and African American youth) but also representing students with exceptionalities (gifted students and those with individual education plans). Three of the respondents discussed the liminality of this experience having a direct impact on their personal cultural experience and practice connecting to the literature on the impact of sustained monocultural realities on White students (Sleeter, 2008).

In my placement I see a lot of resistance in regards to race and sexuality. . . . I think that we are not exposed to enough cultural difference because the school is in a rural area.

CRP Class Integration. When asked about how well culture is integrated into their courses, both HBCU faculty stated that culture is embedded into all classes and experiences within the program. The emerging themes were *integrated* and *travel.* Travel was mentioned here as an added element that is important to the college as a whole, with a study abroad opportunity also specific to the program. HBCU teacher responses aligned with faculty reports also reflecting the same theme *integrated.*

Respondents stated that all classes discussed how to incorporate culture into content and asked students to demonstrate their understanding by integrating culture into assignments in different classes (Hayes & Juarez, 2012). Multicultural education was identified as a course that specifically went in depth to have preservice teachers challenge biases against race, class, gender, ability/disability, sexual orientation, and spirituality/religion. The course description is as follows:

> Given the changing demographics in our country, this course is designed to equip future teachers with fundamental knowledge of understanding culture and teaching children from diverse backgrounds. This course is specifically designed to challenge your personal biases and limiting beliefs in regards to difference, while examining 1) the nature and function of culture; 2) the development of individual and group cultural identities; 3) definitions and implications of diversity, and 4) the influences of culture on learning, development, pedagogy, and outcomes.

Themes for PWI faculty were *intentionality* and *requirements.* Both respondents spoke of program requirements and intentions rather than program-wide infusion. Faculty 1 mentioned two specific classes (Social Curriculum and Children's Literature) and a rubric that is "supposed to be" assessed in each class but not necessarily completed. The identified theme for teacher responses was *some classes.* Teacher participants stated that cultural considerations were integrated into some of their courses—however, only explicitly focused on in Social Curriculum. The course description for Principles of Social Curriculum states:

> This course will acquaint the teacher candidate with relevant classroom community development issues such as care, mutual respect, conflict resolution, motivation, diversity, and developmental assets. Teacher candidates will

investigate philosophical orientations that align to various classroom management practices, and apply them to field experiences in order to develop a workable approach to classroom community development for student success.

The course description does not explicitly state that different aspects of culture or student beliefs and biases will be explored. None of the PWI respondents (faculty or teachers) discussed challenging teacher candidates to explore their own beliefs and practices. The intention to integrate culture is evident here through faculty and teacher responses and the program evaluation; whether it is happening at a meaningful level is in question (Hayes & Juarez, 2012).

Student, Personal, and Other Faculty Resistance. Faculty were next asked to discuss any resistance they have encountered within their programs to discussing culture and diversity. The HBCU faculty theme was *no resistance* for students, other faculty, as well as for themselves. Both respondents stated that they have not experienced any student or faculty resistance to culture and diversity and that they personally did not have any issues with the construct.

Faculty 1 discussed her experience with students being interested in learning more about the impact of diversity in education. This respondent also stated that she attributes the lack of resistance to the cultural nature of HBCUs and possibly to their own feelings of marginalization in their educational experience. This response was in line with the literature (Dilworth, 2012; Lewis & Taylor, 2015; Thompson, 2015a; Young, 2004) and the initial study expectations.

PWI faculty responses and themes were different for student resistance (*resistance* and *lack of exposure*), personal resistance (*fear* and *challenging beliefs*), and other faculty resistance (*resistance, microaggressions,* and *complicity*). Both faculty discussed the negative experiences faculty across the campus (not only within their program) have had when attempting to discuss culture and diversity. They discussed student defensiveness, lack of exposure or homogeneity of experience, misconceptions, and implicit bias in line with the findings of Amos (2016), Sleeter (2008), and Williams and Evans-Winters (2005). Faculty 1 stated:

For years I've heard the response that if we'd just stop talking about it, it wouldn't be an issue. Some students won't share out loud for fear of being persecuted by peers or me as the teacher if they have differing perspectives—I consider that a form of resistance. I often hear, "what's the point" of bringing up an issue if it is not directly happening *to* the student/community. i.e. "WE don't have this [issue]."

Faculty 1 discussed some students as presenting with "an inability to explore issues of culture at a deep level," again connecting back to the issues of lack of exposure and developing within a monocultural vacuum (Lowenstein, 2009; Sleeter, 2008).

> There is also often an assumption that in this area at least, "we all" have "most" cultural things in common. Misconceptions about diversity sometimes result in resistance or inability to explore deeply. The other day students were discussing the value of the religious diversity in their small group, even using the words, "we all have different religions." The "religions" were Catholic, Baptist, and Methodist.

In terms of reporting on their own feelings, both faculty at the PWI discussed fear as a source of personal resistance in terms of alienating students and student retaliation. One discussed questioning her ability to be accurately responsive in "saying just the right thing" during discussions. She also discussed aspects of culture challenging and disrupting her own deeply held beliefs that she has yet to confront. Faculty 2 discussed a fear of being labeled as angry or hysterical by her students. Both responses reflected the fear of "being preyed on" by their students discussed by Amos (2016) found in PWI spaces.

> Resistance inevitably comes whenever we discuss privilege, but most recently, I also experienced resistance and even rejection of considerations of implicit bias. There is a disconnect between what they see as "bad" or "intolerant" views on diversity and the implicit biases evident in their observable actions.

This is part of the reason unpacking privilege is so vital to culture work. Both faculty respondents also discussed other faculty within the program exhibiting implicit bias, White faculty members being expected to be complicit in that bias, Black faculty members experiencing microaggressions from colleagues (that is, refusing to refer to them as doctor but referring to fellow White colleagues solely as doctor so and so), and the pressure and stress related to confrontation when faculty do make the attempt to address bias. This connects back to the findings of Sleeter (2008).

Culture in Instruction. HBCU faculty themes for employing culture in their own personal instructional practices were *every class* and *culture encompassing.* They discussed focusing on aspects of culture very frequently, on a weekly basis, and connecting it to each different course topic. Faculty 2 explained that culture is "all encompassing" or connected to everything.

It comes up often. Since culture is all encompassing, whenever we are talking about students, families, trends, instruction etc. some aspect of culture may come up.

The PWI faculty themes were *weekly* and *modeling*. Both discussed modeling the use of culture weekly in instruction. Faculty 1 connected this practice to good pedagogy and experiential meaning making, which again connects to how deep faculty are actually delving in their discussion of culture and diversity. For instance, Faculty 1 stated:

> Because I am always attempting to model good pedagogy, I am hopefully modeling cultural responsiveness and therefore integrating culture into our weekly class meetings. As part of our conceptual framework, experiential meaning making would regularly require students to use cultural understandings to make meaning.

There is a vast difference between mentioning the word *culture* (providing lip service to the construct) and actually unpacking different manifestations of culture (pushing students' perceived boundaries to challenge deeply held limiting beliefs).

Depth of Diversity in the Program. In this domain, HBCU faculty differed slightly in their responses generating the themes of *varying depth* and *impactful experience*. Faculty 1 discussed providing impactful cultural experiences for teacher candidates and this "taking place at a deep level of processing as culture is embedded in all experiences." Faculty 2 at the HBCU stated that it is discussed at "varying levels of depth depending on the content and focus of the particular lesson." This could be where the transmission of culturally responsive practice can be fine-tuned to ensure that deep processing is consistent across courses and instructors.

The PWI faculty on the other hand demonstrated agreement reflecting the themes of *shallow* and *not impactful*. Faculty reported that culture and diversity are discussed at a shallow level and that the teacher preparation program is making efforts to shift this practice. Faculty 2 stated, "There are some dedicated faculty members whom are attempting to take it to a deeper level." However, Faculty 1 acknowledged that current conversations are "intangible" and "not impactful."

> Without some kind of action, praxis, if you will, I have to think that any discussions are on some level shallow. Therefore, I would say that we're working at a shallow level in the TPP [teacher preparation program] because I can't identify any tangible ways that we are acting on the environment.

Faculty Recommendations for Enhancing CRP Preparation. Through a synthesis of the data provided, cultural considerations appear to have been intentionally infused throughout the HBCU teacher preparation program. Although there were areas that could be strengthened, the program appears to be working toward transforming how their future teachers respond to students with differing backgrounds. Integration was not expected to be found at this level (Hayes & Juarez, 2012; Villegas & Lucas, 2007).

They appear to be working to focus on all aspects of culture and diversity rather than simply dealing with Black students from low socioeconomic status areas as the literature suggests (Dilworth, 2012; Irvine & Fenwick, 2011). This could be partly due to the ease of discussing culture in HBCU spaces. Faculty stated that culturally responsive teacher preparation could be enhanced by "focusing on what culture is" (explicitly defining this for students) and "establishing interstate and global field experiences," generating the themes of *global field experience* and the *what of CRP.*

The PWI appears to be making strides to include culture considerations in the program; however, it currently appears to be treated as supplemental in a number of areas (field experiences, courses, program policies, conceptual framework). Culture might not be fully integrated because of the fear that exists connected to unpacking culture at a deep level and student responses to the process. This was in line with the research (Irvine & Fenwick, 2011; Lowenstein, 2009; Sleeter, 2008) as well as the initial study expectations.

PWI faculty themes for recommendations for enhancing CRP were *diverse faculty, family engagement,* and the *why of CRP.* They suggested that "preparation could be enhanced by the hiring of more diverse faculty to increase exposure to difference, engaging in authentic family engagement, and making sure students explore the why of CRP in order to better understand the impact they might have on their students." There was no mention of focused training for faculty to support them through engaging students and leading difficult conversations or addressing faculty fears, all of which are important aspects of programmatic cultural infusion.

Teacher Attitudes toward CRP

Qualitative research question 2 was concerned with teacher feelings toward culturally responsive pedagogy. This question was explored via teacher questionnaire inquiry responses to numbers 2 (the importance of CRP in classroom outcomes), 6 (feelings of resistance), and 8 (comfort integrating CRP into instruction). This question also provides context to teacher scores on the culturally responsive teacher outcome expectancy scale.

The Importance of CRP in Classroom Outcomes. HBCU teacher responses reflected the themes of *important* and *overcome bias.* Participants discussed CRP as important to setting the foundation for overcoming bias, understanding students, meeting specific needs, establishing deeper connections, and building relationships that allow students to feel included and valued in the educational process. For example, one respondent stated:

> Culturally responsive pedagogy is critical to successful outcome in the classroom. If a teacher is not aware of the type of cultural background of their students there is no way, they are making their classroom a thriving learning environment. Using CRP allows teachers to tailor assignments so that students of all backgrounds feel included.

PWI teacher themes were *important* and *climate of respect.* All of the PWI teacher participants also identified culturally responsive pedagogy as being important to successful outcomes, specifically to expose students to differences, help them make deeper connections, make them feel welcome, and create a climate of respect while developing them into productive citizens.

> I believe that it is important, because all learners deserve to feel that their culture is valued and important. This will allow for a more open and respectful classroom atmosphere, and will aid in establishing learners that are eager to learn and accept cultures other than their own.

Feelings of Resistance toward CRP. HBCU teacher themes for personal resistance were *no resistance* and *importance.* In line with the research (Dilworth, 2012; Lewis & Taylor, 2015), they reported no feelings of resistance to the construct itself, citing connections to their own cultures and an open, growth-focused mind-set, and viewing themselves as global citizens as possible reasons for their perceived level of comfort.

> I don't feel any resistance about this topic. My family's culture has always been present in my life. It's something natural for me to express and discuss it.

Two themes emerged from PWI teacher data regarding personal resistance to CRP: *some resistance* and *no resistance.* Seven of the same PWI teachers who identified CRP as being important also acknowledged feelings of resistance in engaging in cultural conversations, citing lack of experience, wanting to avoid conflict, and not wanting to offend others with differing beliefs as the reasons behind their discomfort (Amos, 2016; Sleeter, 2008; Williams & Evans-Winters, 2005). One teacher stated that "being part of the majority group and holding majority views means she is automatically less open minded in the eyes of others," so she tends to be silent during discussions.

Six respondents said they have "no resistance" but then identified discomfort with discussing certain aspects of culture (that is, LGBTQ, religion). One stated that this discomfort "does not have any impact" on her practice. This reflects a possible disconnect in the acknowledgment of culture and the level of depth of processing of cultural considerations, providing a tangible example of the "inability to explore deeply" mentioned by Faculty respondent 1 (Lowenstein, 2009).

Comfort Integrating CRP into Instruction. HBCU teacher responses generated the themes of *comfortable* and *often*. Respondents indicated that they were extremely to moderately comfortable addressing different aspects of culture during their own instructional practice. Only a few participants stated that they already do this often, challenging bias, and offering alternatives to traditional historical information, so that their students are afforded a different experience from the one they were provided in their own K–12 educational experiences.

> I try to address this in my classroom instruction with students. I let them question their own beliefs and prejudices and then challenge them to consider alternatives.

One moderately comfortable student stated that she was not sure if she knew enough to integrate it during instructional time. Two students attributed their level of comfort to their teacher preparation program. Overall, HBCU teachers appeared to find CRP to be important, necessary, useful, and to some degree doable.

Although most of the PWI teacher participants also discussed feeling comfortable addressing culture in instruction, their resistance and level of preparation was reflected in their answers. Their responses generated the themes of *comfortable* in terms of talking about different cultures and *uncomfortable* in terms of perceived difficulty and just not knowing how to implement CRP practices as the process has not been properly put into context (Ladson-Billings, 2008).

> I do not feel incredibly comfortable mainly because I don't know how to effectively implement it in instruction. How do I teach kids math concepts that they have to learn while also teaching them how to be respectful and productive citizens? We have spent time in class discussing ways to do this, but sometimes the challenge to present CRP in the classroom seems overwhelming.

Table 8.3. Teacher Response Coding Themes and Subthemes

Dimension	HBCU Themes	HBCU Subthemes	PWI Themes	PWI Subthemes
CRP Defined	Incorporate Culture Intentional Planning Bridge Gaps	Student Centered Global Awareness Teach without Bias Differentiation All Aspects of Learning N/A	Asset Oriented Incorporate Culture	Student Directed Personal Connections Student Centered Tolerance Awareness
CRP Importance	Important Overcome Bias	Feel Valued Build Relationships Successful Outcome Deeper Connections Safe Space	Important Climate of Respect	Exposure Feel Welcome Personal Connections Productive Citizens Strong Connections Relationships
FE Diversity	Levels of Diversity Exceptionalities	Ethnicities Socioeconomic Status Type of School N/A	Lack of Diversity Exceptionalities	Rural Monocultural N/A
Class Integration	Integrated	Class Content Activities Implicit/Explicit	Some Classes	Social Curriculum Different Perspectives
Unsafe/Shut Down	Never Safe Space	N/A Push Comfort Zone Open-Minded Professors	Shut Down No	Unpopular Opinion Judged Religion No Explanation Does Not Speak Open Atmosphere

Personal Resistance	No Resistance	N/A	Some Resistance	*Lack of Exposure* *Avoid Conflict* *Differing Opinions*
	Importance	*Global View* *Own Culture*	No Resistance	*Some Discomfort* *No explanation*
Student/ Faculty Resistance	No Student Resistance	N/A	Student Resistance	*Fear* *Lack of Experience*
	No Faculty Resistance	N/A	Faculty Resistance	*Shut Conversation* *Down* *Prejudiced Comment* *Discomfort*
			No	*No Explanation*
Comfort Addressing	Comfortable	*Different Perspectives* *Training* *Benefits*	Comfortable	*Different Perspectives*
	Often	N/A	Uncomfortable	*Don't Know How* *Difficulty/Time*
Depth of Diversity	Deep Discussions	*Outside Experience* *Teaching beyond* *Activities/Events*	Shallow Discussions	*Don't Push Boundary* *Limited Demographic*
	Shallow Secondary	*No Multicultural* *Education*	Deep Some Classes	*Depends on Professor*
Enhancing CRP Prep	Continue	*TPP Doing Good Job*	Specific Class	*Exposure*
	Multicultural Secondary	*Course Option*	Prof. Modeling	*Teach How* *Study Cultures* *CRP Lesson Plans*
			Travel	*Conferences* *Exposure*

Many did not discuss any specific responsive behaviors. Some respondents discussed superficial manifestations of culture (Ladson-Billings, 2014). One response focused on incorporating her own culture in the classroom but did not mention focusing on any of her students' cultures.

Another teacher explicitly stated that her comfort was not aided by her teacher preparation program but by her personal desire for growth. Five teachers said they were uncomfortable because the idea of CRP is overwhelming, difficult, and they do not know how to effectively implement it. One student stated there is "little time for culture in science" because she is attempting to cover required standards. PWI responses showed discrepancy between thought and action in culturally responsive practice (Chu & Garcia, 2014; Siwatu, 2007).

Feelings about culturally responsive practice appeared to be connected to the level of engagement with culture in the program. Outcome expectations are based on both personal experience and the experience of models (Siwatu, 2007). All teacher respondents across institutions appeared to feel as though culturally responsive pedagogy was important to connections with students and positive student outcomes.

However, HBCU-trained teachers appeared to feel like it was more tangible or doable than PWI-trained teachers who reported needing "more development in this area" or not understanding how to integrate it into practice. The HBCU students did not appear to feel it was an insurmountable task. This could be an indication that faculty at the HBCU are doing a better job at modeling the construct than PWI faculty (Chu & Garcia, 2014).

Reflecting on CRP Preparation

The current research on culturally responsive teacher preparation was also concerned with teacher feelings about their own level of preparation provided by their teacher certification programs. This third research question was explored through teacher questionnaire numbers 5 (feeling unsafe or shut down during discussions), 7 (other student or faculty resistance to discussing culture), 9 (depth of diversity in the program), and 10 (teacher suggestions for enhancing CRP prep in the program). These responses provide a glimpse into what is actually taking place as students traverse through the program while providing a springboard toward focused program enhancement.

Feeling Unsafe or Shut Down during Discussions. In terms of the HBCU, the teachers were adamant that they never felt unsafe or shut down during conversations on culture and diversity, yielding the themes of *never* and *safe space.* Teacher responses indicated that their professors consistently took them outside of their comfort zones and pushed them to engage through discomfort within safe spaces where faculty were also willing to share their own experiences and perspectives while keeping an open mind.

> No. All of our professors were very open minded and were genuinely concerned about helping me develop [CRP] teaching strategies.

PWI teacher responses provided a slightly different picture of cultural focus in the preparation program, yielding the themes of *shut down* and simply *no.* Six teachers stated that they were often shut down by professors and sometimes by their fellow colleagues, connecting back to the findings of Lowenstein (2009). Teachers also discussed feeling judged and unheard. This occurred during discussions about culture, religion, race, sexuality, and traditions.

> Unsafe, no, however feeling shut down has occurred. This occurs often because of difference of opinions between the group or with the professor. This has happened a number of times in group discussions, but mostly because there is a shift away from the student's specific view on the topic. I do not believe it is intentional, but I still feel as though it occurs.

> There have been a few times in the program where I knew my opinion would be judged or taken the wrong way.

Respondents discussed censoring their responses, shutting down, and remaining silent when sensing professor disapproval as well as "when discussions became unproductive." Seven participants said they did not feel shut down. Four offered no explanation, two reported being open-minded, and one said she does not voice her opinion so there is no opportunity for her to be shut down. This speaks to the level of depth of processing of culture in the program overall as well as the need to contextualize and unpack cultural conversations in a supportive and competent fashion (Ladson-Billings, 2008).

Other Student or Faculty Resistance to Discussing Culture. HBCU responses reflected the themes of *no student resistance* and *no faculty resistance* to pushing through culture-based conversations. It is worthy of note that all of the respondents said this was not their experience. One student stated that "being at an HBCU makes conversations about culture easier because the other students share some of the same characteristics."

PWI teacher responses on the other hand generated the themes of *student resistance* and *faculty resistance.* Four of the teachers simply answered no to this question with no explanation provided. Nine of the teachers discussed witnessing resistance in both other students and faculty members. They stated that students feared unpopular opinions and professors with differing views reported heated discussions and lack of experience. One teacher discussed faculty having specific resistance to the issues of race and sexuality, while a number of students experienced professors changing the subject and shutting down discussions (Amos, 2016).

> Yes. While there are similar beliefs in our group, there are some things that can be of a touchy subject for both students and faculty. There have been some things that faculty shuts down because they do not want to discuss it or they do not believe it. Conversations have been steered in a different direction quickly.

> Not in the classroom to the person's face during a discussion. I have noticed that some people will discuss their opinions outside of the classroom with someone else to not make the other person mad at their beliefs.

Depth of Diversity in the Program. HBCU teacher responses yielded the themes of *deep discussions* and *shallow secondary.* Teachers reported that many of the diversity discussions they had in the program were processed at a deep and meaningful level. One teacher stated, "The fact that I am able to apply my knowledge from the program to my own teaching experience now, shows that I was able to gain an immense amount from the program."

Two students explained that discussions may be somewhat shallow for secondary students who are not able to take the multicultural education course that delves deeper into diversity. The issue with secondary students is well known and experienced in programs nationally. This is due to major restrictions and scheduling conflicts/time constraints as these students are essentially double majors receiving content from their subject concentration and methods from education departments.

PWI teacher themes for depth of diversity were *shallow discussions* (mirroring faculty reports) and *deep for some classes.* Most of the PWI teacher respondents agreed with faculty reports that culture is discussed at a shallow level in the program. Similar to Sleeter (2008), the few participants who said it was deep also attributed this to one professor and one specific course (again social curriculum). One respondent gave a contradictory response:

> I feel we have approached a deep level of talking about diversity. However, many of our discussions are on a shallow level. I feel diversity is well known and discussed topic though. I believe we try to dig deep into the topic; however, we do not overstep any boundaries.

Teachers said culture is discussed as important but they do not have much experience with it and are not expressly taught how to integrate it into instruction. Culture and diversity appear to be discussed at some length; however, teachers felt that their own culture is rarely discussed, professors do not push boundaries, and they tend to avoid controversial topics (Lowenstein, 2009, Ladson-Billings, 2008).

Teacher Suggestions for Enhancing CRP Preparation in the Program. HBCU teacher recommendations to enhance culturally responsive preservice teaching preparation in the HBCU program reflected the themes of *continue* and *multicultural for secondary.* Suggestions included more small group discussions to alleviate pressure and anxieties, a focused diversity course at each level of the program (each year), and more in-depth conversations that include all faculty and staff in the program with cooperating teachers from placement sites. Many of the teacher respondents expressed satisfaction with their program as is and urged faculty to continue doing the work. Teachers stated that the program did not ignore culture and that it pushed them to grow as educators.

I do not have any suggestions or recommendations. I believe that the teacher preparation program at my institution has been very in depth.

PWI teachers themes were *specific class, professor modeling,* and *travel.* Teachers stated that culturally responsive preparation could be enhanced in a number of ways. First, a class should be added that deals with specific cultures allowing preservice teachers to explore other beliefs, opinions, and cultures without being shut down. Second, culture should be incorporated into all classes in the program.

Third, faculty should keep an open mind and consistently model culturally responsive behaviors for students. Lastly, students should be allowed to travel, attend conferences, and be exposed to other cultures so that they can engage with culture in more meaningful ways. Their responses matched previous research findings (Siwatu, 2007; Zhao, Meyers, & Meyers, 2009).

Teach preservice teachers how to integrate the pedagogy every day rather than every once in a while.

Allowing students to speak their mind and to dissect what they have said instead of continually arguing would definitely allow for more [CRP] skills. Because our college is placed in such a culturally similar area it would benefit us greatly to take trips or experience teaching in other areas.

Table 8.4. Teacher Contextual CRP Response Themes and Subthemes

Dimension	HBCU Themes	HBCU Subthemes	PWI Themes	PWI Subthemes
Question 1: ELL Students	Assess Language	Differentiate	Assess Language	Differentiate
	Bilingual Approach	Indigenous Language	Bilingual Approach	Indigenous Language
	Build Relationship	Support Family Communication	Build Relationship	Learn Background Classroom Communication
Question 2: Latinx/Indigenous	Incorporate Culture	Indigenous Language Cultural Activities Student Centered	Climate of Respect	Build Relationship
	Classroom Communication	Inclusion Safe Space Build Relationship	Build Relationship	Learn Community Welcoming
	Family Communicate	Family Involvement	Incorporate Culture	N/A
Question 3: LGBTQIA+	Intervene	Discuss Bullying Discipline	Intervene	Discuss Bullying Discuss Impact Pull Administration In
	Build Community	Understand Difference Safe Supportive Space Time Together	Build Relationships	Teach Tolerance Time Together
	Connections	Ballet and Sports Interests	Connections	Ballet and Sports Interests
Question 4: Parent Engagement	Important	N/A	Important	N/A
	Communication	Call/Text Regular Communication Pos. Communication	Communication	Parent Night Connection Letters Regular Communication
	Invite In	N/A		

Experiential CRP Responses

Teacher responses to cultural simulations provided an additional glimpse into how the teachers think about culture. They also provided insight into how they might possibly integrate cultural considerations into their practice in certain situations, thus providing a tangible picture of how they have been prepared to engage with cultural scenarios. Overall teachers offered good suggestions across the two institutions (see table 8.3 for themes by institution).

Respondents from both spaces focused on building classroom community and including language through a bilingual approach as vital aspects of working with English language learners. HBCU-trained teachers included family communication to reach students. HBCU respondents also included language of origin for Latinx and Indigenous youth, and both HBCU and PWI participants looked to the community to provide a context for understanding how to work with the youth in the classroom.

A few of the PWI teachers left these questions blank, stating a need for further development in this area. All of the teachers across institutions said they would intervene in the LGBTQIA+ scenario by discussing bullying. Many teachers from both groups said they would build relationships between the youth and also connect dancing to sports and discuss the value in differing interests.

Only PWI teachers (three) said they would bring administration in to deal with the situation, which could be an indicator of some discomfort. In terms of parent engagement, respondents from both institutions focused on regular/consistent communication, relaying the positive and areas for growth, and inviting parents in for parent nights, game nights, or curriculum nights. HBCU participants included calling and texting parents as an added form of personalized communication.

These responses show that students know what to say. They can provide the desired textbook responses that professors might want them to give. Their overall responses, however, show that they treat these considerations as secondary in their own practice. Compartmentalization in training begets compartmentalization in practice. The following chapter provides a quick explanation of how the numbers and the narratives converge to provide a complete picture of culturally responsive teacher preparation for sustaining practice.

~

CHAPTER NINE

A Tale of Two
Differing Programs Continued

Convergence or Divergence

Numbers have an important story to tell. They rely on you to give them a clear and convincing voice.

—Stephen Few

Obstacles do not block the path. They are the path.

—Zen Proverb

Introduction

For the current study, qualitative and quantitative methods were equally prioritized during data collection. Data was collected simultaneously in a single phase, analyzed separately, and then merged here in the interpretation of the results. The following is the mixed method spotlight via a pragmatic lens.

Onwuegbuzie and Collins (2007) discuss the crises of representation and integration in relation to accurately capturing the lived experiences of study participants and combining results in a way that honors the original goals of the research. The research goals were to add to the knowledge base on culturally sustaining practice, to understand complex phenomena, and eventually to have institutional and social impact. The research objectives were exploration and explanation of this phenomenon that seems to be evading practice.

The purpose of the research was to seek convergence of findings, to examine overlapping aspects of the phenomenon, and to address the question surrounding the application of CRP. Or rather why it is not being applied in practice. The following integration of quantitative and qualitative findings is presented in an attempt to mitigate these concerns by showing how the qualitative findings support and expand on the quantitative scores (focusing on avoiding incorrect connections and inferences) and by connecting these findings back to current research on HBCU and PWI spaces in general leading to the ultimate goal: transforming teacher preparation and changing the education system.

Merging the Findings

Connections between the two data strands reflect an overall convergence in quantitative and qualitative findings. At the first point of convergence, the HBCU-trained teachers received slightly higher mean scores on the three measures CRTPS (HBCU μ = 80.462, PWI μ = 66.462), the CRTSE (HBCU μ = 374.308, PWI μ= 329.762), and the CRTOE (HBCU μ = 240.369, PWI μ = 221.092), reflecting the comfort emerging from qualitative findings. HBCU teachers provided responses indicating a greater level of culturally responsive teacher preparation.

In summation of the qualitative points, in comparison with their PWI counterparts, HBCU-prepared teachers provided and reported

- a richer range of definitions of culturally responsive pedagogy,
- more diverse field experiences,
- a greater class integration of culture,
- no personal resistance to unpacking culture,
- no resistance from other students or faculty,
- more comfort integrating culture into their instruction,
- a greater depth of discussion of diversity, and
- being prepared in a more open and challenging environment.

Hayes and Juarez (2012) discussed finding monocultural practices centered in Whiteness across institution type. This was expected to be evident in the study findings at both the HBCU and the PWI. Quantitative results slightly diverged showing both schools working to incorporate culture. Slightly is used here because this does not mean that Whiteness is not apparent in practice at either institution. The HBCU is, however, doing a better job of integrating the construct on a more personal level for preservice teachers. This was reflected in qualitative responses as the program analysis revealed greater integration at the HBCU.

Teacher respondents also reported a deeper level of focus on culture at the HBCU than teachers trained at the PWI who mostly stated that it tended to be shallow, with one professor known for providing a deeper level of discussion. The program analysis indicated that there are faculty who advocate for responsive practices; however, a smaller number of faculty see it as essential or actually incorporate it into their practice. This was supported by faculty interview responses reporting faculty resistance, microaggressions, and implicit bias, as well as teacher responses reporting being shut down by professors during culture-based discussions.

Qualitative results diverged from current research on HBCU teacher preparation but converged for PWI experience in terms of field experiences. Whereas the research reports most field experiences in HBCU spaces taking place in low socioeconomic status and phenotypically similar environments (Dilworth, 2012; Irvine & Fenwick, 2011), both HBCU faculty and teachers reported very diverse placements where preservice teachers are placed with students across the cultural spectrum (race, class, different language learners, exceptionalities) with varying socioeconomic statuses. PWI faculty and teachers, on the other hand, all reported monocultural experiences lacking in real diversity.

Quantitative results converged with qualitative results regarding PWI teacher discomfort in discussing and unpacking culture. The PWI had a lower mean than the HBCU for each of the DVs, which would reflect discomfort in dealing with specific aspects of culture (curriculum and instruction, relationship establishment, and group belonging formation), lower self-efficacy scores, as well as less positive outcome expectations. Between-subject effects of the MANOVA show that the variance in scores for self-efficacy and outcome expectations exist but are not significant.

Overall PWI teachers reported feeling that CRP is important on qualitative measures. This merges with quantitative results as some of the PWI teachers reported feeling comfortable with the construct (although many also reported having feelings of resistance and admitted that they did not know exactly how to apply it). Again, PWI responses showed a mismatch between how teachers are thinking about culture and their actual culturally responsive practice. This connects to Pajares (1996) as results demonstrate that discussion of a concept does not necessarily translate into implementation in practice.

Quantitative results converged with qualitative results regarding the comfort level of HBCU-trained teachers in engaging with culture. HBCU teachers received higher scores indicating more comfort with specific aspects of culture, slightly higher self-efficacy, and more positive outcome expectations than PWI-trained teachers. Specifically, CRTPS subscale scores revealed a higher level of comfort in tweaking curriculum and altering instruction to be more culturally responsive, comfort in establishing optimal relationships with their diverse students, as well as comfort in establishing a classroom community optimal for development in school and the global community.

Again, as between-subject effects show that the variance in scores for self-efficacy and outcome expectations are not significant, a few of the HBCU teachers reported feeling only moderately comfortable. Scale scores reflected this as teachers scored lower for curriculum and instruction than they did on the scales dealing with connecting to students. On the other side, many PWI respondents report feeling very comfortable. Similarly, the contextual CRP-based questions also did not indicate much of a difference in responsive thought processes between teachers trained in both programs.

For instance, teachers from both institutions discussed building classroom community and including language through a bilingual approach as vital aspects of working with English language learners. This correlates to the higher scores both institutions received on the CRTPS group belonging formation subscale and the lower scores received for curriculum and instruction. This may denote a difference between understanding how to incorporate these practices or whether teachers truly think it is of value to do so.

Griffin (2002) and Hilliard (1997) discuss the importance of deep-level processing in terms of culture for preservice teachers, leading to the way that they interact with and the skills they employ with students. The HBCU findings reflected this importance as faculty and teacher respondents reported programmatic integration and deep-level discussions. The PWI findings converged as faculty and teacher responses identified a shallow level of engagement with culture, and some teacher responses reflected superficial manifestations of culture as culture.

Teacher findings regarding self-efficacy converged for HBCU respondents who reflected a high belief in their capabilities to organize and execute culturally responsive practice (Bandura, 1997) on both the CRTSE and their qualitative questionnaires. PWI responses converged with lower CRTSE scores and the ambiguity and discomfort reflected in their questionnaire responses. Bandura (1977) defined outcome expectations as "a person's estimate that a given behavior will lead to certain outcomes" (p. 193). Outcome expectations appeared to be questionable across institutions.

HBCU quantitative and qualitative responses diverged as teachers scored higher in this domain on the CRTOE; however, questionnaire responses show that although they appear confident in the ability to be responsive, they are not employing CRP in practice consistently. According to Bandura

(1986), HBCU teachers reflect the affective response of self-assurance and a moderate behavioral response between high engagement and withdrawal. PWI findings converged on quantitative and qualitative response sets as students scored lower on the CRTOE and also reported lower outcome expectations based on not knowing how to effectively integrate culture.

This connects to research trends in underpreparation and supplemental treatment of culture (Siwatu, 2007). PWI teachers reflected an affective response between self-assurance and self-devaluation and leaned more toward a behavioral response of withdrawal from engagement. In essence, these teachers feel culture is important to focus on but do not see how it can effectively be integrated into practice.

The discriminant function analysis indicated good predictive capacity in estimating whether a respondent was trained at the HBCU ($^{12}/_{13}$) or PWI ($^{9}/_{13}$) based on their perceived level of preparedness, level of self-efficacy, and outcome expectations. This connected to the PWI responses that indicated more comfort than their peers in qualitative responses, making flipped determination of program affiliation more ambiguous. If this were applied to the qualitative coding process (see table 8.3), coders might be able to predict which program teachers were trained in based off of themes found in answers, specifically as related to resistance, field experiences, class integration, and depth of diversity.

The results presented here indicate that there are some good things happening in both institutions and there is work to do in both contexts. Even when teachers scored higher or offered more robust explanations, they were still not integrating sustaining strategies within their own practice. There is a disconnect between theory and practice that can be explained by the focus of training. Lines can be drawn from teacher training to the issues discussed in chapters 1 and 2.

The next chapter considers the implications of these findings. This picture of teacher preparation provides information for where the transformation needs to begin. It offers suggestions for how to revamp teacher preparation in order to train the type of educators needed to bring much needed change to American society. The ingredients needed to nurture super teachers are presented.

$\sim$

Remixing Teacher Education

Shaking Foundations/Building New Structures— Creating Tomorrow's Super Teacher

Each of us is a seed of divinely inspired possibility which when nurtured in our proper context, can and will grow into the fullest expression of all we are supposed to become.

—Dr. Wade G. Nobles

We need teachers with deep belief in the potential of *all* children and a vision for defying expectations.

—Teach for All

Every child can learn.

—Asa G. Hilliard III

Introduction

This chapter presents a discussion of the findings from the study presented in the previous chapter, which are used as a springboard for recommendations for future directions in culturally sustaining practice. Beginning with a summary of content presented in the previous chapters, information is then presented in terms of the study findings and their intersection with the current literature in this area. The overall implications for the development of teacher preparation are presented.

The discussion ends with suggestions for future research and work to create a workable model of culturally sustaining teacher preparation. This model is to be dynamic and have the potential to produce replicable outcomes in multiple and differing environments. The goal is to engender positive outcomes for students of all cultural and socioeconomic backgrounds, which will trickle out into society.

The system absolutely cannot remain as it is. To be 100 percent clear, the education system as it currently stands and as it has been functioning for the past 270 years is inadequate, and it continues to harm students. People do not always think about the fact that teachers hold the future in their hands and have an impact on what it will look like. The world literally depends on how (methods) and what (curriculum) is taught to the children who will be in charge of the future.

Their training does not begin in graduate or trade school when they hone in on a particular path. Training begins in their formative years when educators help to shape

- values (who is worthy and what matters),
- self-efficacy beliefs (their ability to achieve given tasks),
- global perceptions (how and where they fit on the world stage),
- racial beliefs (inclusivity or hatred),
- sociocultural perspectives (ideas about class and community),
- metacognition (how they think about their thinking),
- advocacy and social justice (action or inaction),
- beliefs about meaningful contributions from historical figures and different communities (colonizing or decolonizing history), and
- ideas about what is and what is not possible.

This book is a serious call for attention and actionable change.

Summary of the Study

The purpose of the study was to explore how teacher preparation programs are preparing preservice teachers to engage with the culture of their future students within the process of providing instruction. The expectation was that preparation in this area is not adequate given current treatment of diverse students (Henfield & Washington, 2012; Smith & Harper, 2015; Thompson, 2015b) and national student outcomes (National Assessment of Educational Progress, 2015). Previous chapters discussed the reasons behind the marginalization of children of color in the education system focusing on disidentification based on cultural mistrust and exclusion. This was connected to a synopsis of the original and current research on culturally responsive pedagogy (in its various forms and iterations from 1995 to the present) and how this concept is mostly missing from teacher preparation, as most of the interventions presented in research are focused on existing classroom environments. The point is made that true, consistent, and replicable responsive/sustaining practice would need to begin in teacher preparation programs as it entails an intricate constructive process of working through limiting beliefs that can hinder the consideration of different practices as relevant (Hsaio, 2015; Ladson-Billings, 2014).

In order to present the foundational issues in culturally responsive teacher preparation, the literature review began with the history of education in the United States. American education initially included a de facto exclusion of different cultures because of segregation, then an intentional exclusion of culture in desegregation (Bennet, 2015; Boykin, 2000; Young, 2004). The traditional structure of teacher education was presented, which continues the status quo of cultural exclusion due to monocultural experiences and the realities of K–12 and collegiate education.

Challenges in the current educational landscape of the United States in terms of culture were then presented, specifically educational outcomes for youth from different backgrounds punctuated by current NAEP scores. These youth are experiencing marginality partly due to the exclusion of culture from curriculum and the lack of culturally responsive practice.

In order to present a complete picture of what is currently taking place in teacher preparation specifically related to culturally responsive practice, a convergent parallel mixed methods study was conducted (Creswell, 2014; Onwuegbuzie & Collins, 2007) and presented in chapters 7 through 9. Quantitative analyses included a one-way MANOVA, accompanying assumptions, and discriminant analysis as a post hoc test. There were three dependent variables for the MANOVA: the Culturally Responsive Teacher Preparation Scale (CRTPS), the Culturally Responsive Teacher Self-Efficacy Scale (CRTSE), and the Culturally Responsive Teacher Outcome Expectancy Scale (CRTOE).

The independent variable for the analysis was institution type with two levels: HBCU and PWI. This study particularly highlights issues that exist within teacher preparation in rural and monoethnic environments as they pertain to the transmission of culturally responsive teacher preparation. Both contexts are located at opposite ends of the school spectrum and thus are expected to present pointed challenges to diverse cultural engagement in relation to other more urban environments. This is also an area that is lacking in the research.

Qualitative analyses included a program evaluation, a teacher question-naire, and faculty interviews. The focus of study for each program was student outcome data, course offerings and descriptions, field experience/placement information, program mission/vision/conceptual framework, fac-ulty expertise and research, and anecdotal evidence. Thirteen teachers who received their training from each preparation program (twenty-six in total) participated in the study.

Two faculty members from each institution participated in interviews to provide another layer of context to teacher responses on the three scales (the CRTPS, CRTSE, and CRTOE), teacher questionnaire responses, and the program analysis. This information was analyzed separately (quantitative then qualitative) in chapters 7 and 8. Results were then merged in a mixed method conversation of the results in chapter 9, culminating in the follow-ing discussion.

Limitations

The study had a few minor limitations that were all able to be accounted for by the overall study design. The theoretical frame of pragmatism is eclectic, allowing for the merging of multiple forms of data, but care had to be taken to make sure data did not get lost within the eclecticism. There was a lot of data that had to be tracked and accounted for.

Similarly, the flexible nature of thematic analysis, which makes it an appropriate choice to pair with pragmatism and mixed methodology, also presents with the need to be conscientious so that important data does not become glossed over during the coding process. This was satisfied through the six-step analysis and the employment of multiple raters. A higher score could have been captured for interrater reliability if fewer were employed; however, it was more salient to determine whether multiple people were see-ing the same phenomenon than it was to have a higher rating.

The convergent parallel mixed method design required equal sample sizes in the merging of results, as did MANOVA. This provided a challenge during data collection in making sure that there was accurate representa-tion and that there was an equal number of complete responses. Participants were drawn from a convenience sample of teachers who were trained at each program; however, an initial attempt was made to collect more data than was necessary and randomly include response sets in the study analysis to overcome this limitation.

The design required a lot of data to be collected, and some participants tapped out, leaving a number of unfinished responses and just the right amount of complete responses to garner sufficient power for the study. Care had to be taken in the reporting of MANOVA results to avoid ambiguity and to accurately identify actual effects of the independent variable, avoiding misinterpretation of interaction effects along the dependent variables. MANOVA is limited because it is a more complicated test than running an analysis of variance or ANOVA; however, MANOVA offers more power/protection than running multiple ANOVAs.

Lastly, particular care needed to be taken in the merging and interpretation of the mixed method results. It was of prime concern to ensure understanding of how these different types of data converge to provide a better picture of CRP preparation. The mixed methodology accounted for weaknesses found in the quantitative or qualitative analyses alone.

Findings and Conclusions

As previously discussed, Renner et al. (2004) assert that teacher preparation programs are shirking their responsibility to mold preservice teachers into global citizens living in a diverse world. Findings for the PWI were consistent with this view and the research overall showing that diverse cultures are treated as supplemental to the mandatory curriculum and superficially glossed over during teacher preparation (Hsaio, 2015; Ladson-Billings, 2014; Renner et al., 2004; Villegas & Lucas, 2007). Teachers and faculty both reported that one course (social curriculum) or a few (unnamed) classes focused on diversity.

They also reported that conversations about culture were taking place, but at a surface level. Students were not pushed out of their comfort zones, and were at times shut down by professors in culture-based conversations who seemed to be uncomfortable with the topic.

This also connects to preparation programs centering practice in whiteness (Hayes & Juarez, 2012) and how this trend perpetuates the dismissal of culture and feelings of resistance.

In line with Amos (2016), Evans-Winters (2005), and Sleeter (2008) this trend showed up in the data as both teachers and faculty reported experiencing resistance from students and fellow professors. One of the PWI faculty stated:

I often hear, "what's the point of bringing up an issue if it is not directly happening" to the student/community. Students will say "*we* don't have that issue."

According to faculty report, the PWI students tended to view issues surrounding culture as separate and foreign problems that do not pertain to them. This treatment can lend itself to the process of othering culturally diverse and low socioeconomic status students. This othering is dangerous when taken out into real-world contexts.

The HBCU program appears to be making strides to counter this practice by intentionally integrating culture throughout the curriculum and guiding students through the process of challenging their existing biases and limiting beliefs (Villegas & Lucas, 2007; Hayes & Juarez, 2012). The program also goes against the grain of typical HBCU preparation that tends to center field experience in low socioeconomic and phenotypically similar spaces (Dilworth, 2012; Irvine & Fenwick, 2011). The faculty purposefully provide placements that offer experience with multiple levels of diversity (low and high socioeconomic status, urban and suburban, single gender, coed, international, multilingual, private, charter, public, etc.).

While this particular institution as a whole has recently become known and highlighted for student international travel, the program has also created an international travel opportunity specifically for preservice teachers to experience schooling in another country and cultural context. Counter to Bakari (2003), HBCU-trained teachers reported comfort in working with students with different cultural backgrounds. They also stated that they did not experience any resistance from fellow students or faculty members allowing for trust establishment and deeper exploration.

Teachers from both institutions are not adequately or consistently integrating culture into their own personal classroom practice (Gay, 2002; Matthews et al., 2010; McIntyre, 1996). This is the case although integration is taking place on a deeper level at the HBCU than at the PWI. HBCU-trained teachers reported a higher level of comfort employing culturally responsive practice (specifically related to relationship establishment and group belonging formation), however reports are not necessarily meeting up with reality.

In line with the research, this indicates that the teachers' beliefs in their ability to apply what they have learned in their teaching practice is shaky (Bandura, 1977; Bandura, 1997; Pajares, 1996; Siwatu, 2007, 2011). This is directly connected to how they have been trained to think about and engage with culture (Chu & Garcia, 2014; Hsaio, 2015; Ladson-Billings, 2014; Renner et al., 2004; Siwatu, 2007). Or rather, how they have *not* been trained to put it into practice.

All teacher respondents across institutions scored low on the curriculum and instruction subscale of the culturally responsive teacher preparation scale. This indicates that they feel less prepared to integrate culture into their instruction (Hsaio, 2015; Ladson-Billings, 2014; Renner et al., 2004; Siwatu, 2007; Villegas & Lucas, 2007). In essence, comfort with and base understanding of theory is not translating into their personal practice.

Teacher responses connect with multiple reports of current educational practices (Amos, 2016; Bass & Coleman, 1997; Berry, 2003; Lowenstein, 2009; Parsons, 2003; Renner et al., 2004). It has come down to the fact that further development is needed in both spaces, at the PWI and the HBCU, on multiple levels. As Pajares (1996) discusses, the results of the study also show that the acquisition of basic knowledge (mentioning culture or saying culture is important) in a certain area does not translate into competence in that area or predict future implementation once teachers are in charge of their own classrooms. This leads directly into implications for the study and the potential future of teacher preparation programs.

Implications

So where does this leave us? Overall, the profession must stop providing lip service to the terms *culture* and *diversity*. This takes place in multiple programs and professional educational organizations. Everyone is talking about culture these days simply because it is the thing to do. The reality is that not many are actually *doing* it.

Dixson and Fasching-Varner (2009) state that the acknowledgment of culture in instruction equates to the belief in the "fundamental humanity" of students. This view is shared and championed here. Incorporating multiple truths mitigates marginalization, demonstrates caring, facilitates the formation of positive relationships, facilitates meaningful connections to content, and engenders positive academic outcomes for all children (Irving & Hudley, 2008; Hsaio, 2015; Kalyanpur & Harry, 1997; Kea & Utley, 1998; Ladson-Billings, 2000, 2006; Renner et al., 2004; Singh, 2011; Villegas & Lucas, 2002; Young, 2004; Zhao, Meyers, & Meyers, 2009).

These positive connections could also attract more people of color to the teaching profession, shifting the gap in teacher diversity (Amos, 2016; U.S. Department of Education, 2016). Shifting the mandatory curriculum, providing more teacher autonomy in the delivery of instruction and assessment, and providing more administrator support will serve to reconnect teachers to the love of educating and create more pockets of happiness within the profession. A number of our teachers are struggling and just plain unhappy and overwhelmed. The culture of testing needs to be purged and replaced for the well-being of teachers and for the sake of the children.

Exposing all children to the successes and cultural truths stemming from different backgrounds within the curriculum will not only engender a more solid grasp of content, it will also influence their belief in the "fundamental humanity" of all people rather than just those who exemplify certain characteristics. Developing teacher preparation has real potential to positively impact the larger society because of the quality of the individuals this will produce and send out to all professions.

Thus, true participation in culturally sustaining preparation and demonstration of communicative competency (Crago et al., 1997) should be made consequential to the completion of teaching degrees and graduation. As previously discussed, CAEP accreditation standards (2015) require diversity to be threaded through preparation programs, but again CAEP does not provide explicit examples of how this should be done, and the results of this study show that it is not happening at the level that it should. If students do not demonstrate understanding of content or assessment, they cannot become certified to teach or graduate from their program.

They do not learn these things in the process of teaching, they are prerequisites for certification and teaching. The same should become true for demonstrating cultural competence, patience with students who present differently, and a consistent ability to deliver sustaining lessons. Part of the reason students remain marginalized is that cultural competence is a hot button phrase rather than a requirement, and those who do attempt integration are taking on this monumental task alone while leading a classroom, so it becomes an overwhelming chore that more often than not becomes abandoned in the process of meeting district standards.

Focus during preservice training ensures that everyone prioritizes sustaining practice as a given element of instruction, learns how to integrate culture into lesson planning, and understands how to actually implement responsive lessons during content delivery. Making it a mandatory transition point of program completion will make it second nature and a part of what it means to teach rather than just one more thing teachers are asked to do. It will become akin to good teaching practice.

This entails a continuous and constructive process in which students would need to be guided through the process of shedding the veil of their own beliefs (throwing out old and potentially harmful schema) in order to incorporate the possibility that the cultural ways of being of others are valid and real. This allows for the integration of schema based on the acknowledgment and respect of difference (Hamza & Hahn, 2012; Ormrod, 2014). They would also have to understand that this acknowledgment does not negate or counter their own beliefs.

This was a fear that showed up in the current study data from PWI faculty (teacher trainers). Confronting potentially limiting beliefs would simply expand their thinking and validate the existence of their students, adding positively to their practice (Hsaio, 2015; Ladson-Billings, 2014). This is not happening currently, partly because the faculty at various institutions are not themselves comfortable with the concept of culture because they have not gone through the process of challenging their own personal bias and adopting sustaining practice either (Hilliard, 1992).

This was evident in PWI teacher and faculty responses for the current study. It is not that White students are deficient leaners in this area by any stretch of the imagination as discussed in Lowenstein (2009). The issue is rather that they are not being exposed and they are not being taught. They are not being taught about other cultures. They are not being taught that other cultures are relevant. They are not taught adequately how to engage with culture (Hayes & Juarez, 2012; Sleeter, 2008). Nor are they being guided in how to shed existing bias, endure discomfort, or develop competency (Ladson-Billings, 2014).

This trend arose from PWI faculty and teacher data. One of the PWI faculty shared that she is hesitant to engage in some culture-based conversations because they challenge her own deeply held beliefs. This may reveal that she and other professors need more work in challenging their own personal biases before guiding students through the process. PWI teachers discussed professors shutting down culture-based discussions. The indication is that the preparers need to be better prepared. The trainers themselves need to be trained.

Training will allow us to confront the reality of Whiteness that permeates teacher education. Whiteness stems from monocultural educational experiences in K–12 and college. It is then cycled through and played out in teacher education because it is ingrained as the standard. It is ingrained as the standard regardless of cultural background, so it is perpetuated in all schooling environments.

This harmful foundation has to be delicately demolished and replaced with multiple perspectives. The word *delicate* is purposefully used here because Whiteness is attached to deeply held beliefs that many fight to hold on to. It has to be challenged with care and sincerity. It is difficult to see anyone or anything else through the wall of Whiteness that is blocking progress in the system and causing harm as it keeps White students from seeing anyone else and students of color from truly being able to see themselves.

Keeping this in mind, here is the charge. All faculty who teach preservice teachers need to engage in continuous deep-level diversity trainings, first taking them through the process they will lead their students through, then learning how to effectively guide students through the process of challenging bias and participating in difficult conversations. They need to learn this in ways that acknowledge the spectrum of responses and feelings that might accompany confronting beliefs without alienating, attacking, and shutting students down.

Faculty would need to become comfortable with sitting in discomfort with students. Then they must learn how to process and debrief discomfort experienced by their students. This will also assist with full program integration as all faculty would be capable of engaging in, leading, and debriefing deep-level conversation on varying topics. This should not be considered to be the job of one dedicated faculty member but *all* faculty in teacher preparation. The key also lies in this taking place on a continuing basis.

Safe spaces for discussing cultural difference need to be further developed into brave spaces (Arao & Clemens, 2013). The space is safe because information is not shared beyond the group and students are specifically informed that they will be challenged and they will feel dis-ease, or disequilibrium, and that all of this means that transformational growth is taking place. They need to feel supported and guided through this process so that they do not develop further resistance or an aversion to culture.

The space is also brave because they will be made to feel comfortable and safe enough to push through anger and frustration that can arise when engaging in such work. They will not feel threatened by these feeling but more self-aware of what their existence means for them personally. Feelings must be fully addressed and processed before anyone leaves the classroom and then addressed again to make sure the process is scaffolded and that there are no lingering negative feelings.

They cannot be allowed to remain resistant and defensive. They have to understand coming into the program that they will be required to participate in this process. This should be a part of the process of becoming a teacher. This title should carry with it a greater responsibility and level of specificity as to its meaning. Preservice teachers must be invited to participate in their own growth and move beyond tolerance to acknowledgment and acceptance.

To tolerate is to be capable of continued *subjection* to difference. To accept is to receive as adequate, as relevant, and as necessary. The variance between these terms is the difference between just getting through something or allowing it to exist and actually embracing the concept.

Many of the PWI-trained teachers in the study spoke specifically of tolerating difference, demonstrating surface-level engagement with culture. As Ladson-Billings (2008) discusses, the cultural conversation at the PWI is not being placed into context for students who are left feeling frustrated and confused not knowing how to process this new information. The process has become oppositional for them and has caused cognitive dissonance.

This leads to students feeling defensive, destabilized, and extremely uncomfortable in discussing and dealing with culture (Amos, 2016; Griffin, 2002; Lowenstein, 2009), so they simply choose not to deal with it. They choose comfort over progress. It needs to be explicitly stated that in this practice, they choose themselves over their students.

Part of the remedy for this would absolutely include exposure to difference through travel, national/international field exchanges/experiences, and residential field exchange and weekend trips for rural-based educator programs as exposure heightens understanding (Renner et al., 2004; Zhao, Meyers, & Meyers, 2009). The other part of this would take place in a course with the specific purpose of providing the space for students to experience, challenge, process, push, and grow before they have the opportunity to affect young lives. According to the data, this appears to be taking place on a small level at the HBCU, specifically in the multicultural class and bleeding over and coursing through multiple other courses, but lacking at any rate of depth at the PWI.

This is problematic. As Sleeter (2008) states, White students have to mitigate the impact of ongoing, everyday, homogenous, and monoculturally curricular schooling experiences from K–12 through college to teaching. They also need to palliate the banking model of teaching and learning experienced and perpetuated every day in classrooms. This concern showed up in the PWI responses as respondents specifically mentioned lack of exposure and monocultural experiences.

Mitigation will not happen through disjointed conversations but must take place in dedicated spaces, with professors who are specifically trained to challenge them and guide them through it. In order for this to be continuous and thorough work, there needs to be a funding stream (line item) added specifically for culturally responsive preparation (Dilworth, 2012; Irvine & Fenwick, 2011) to support this work. Allocated funds would provide support for specific faculty trainings beyond national conference attendance.

The reality is that faculty do not necessarily engage with culture in these spaces. There would need to be a number of trainings to transform thinking and comfort levels. This funding stream would also support student exposure to difference in the form of national and international travel, bringing in speakers for culture-based workshops, conferences, field trips, domestic exchange, and culturally enhanced field experiences.

Once culture and difference have been engaged with meaningfully and responsibly, methods instructors need to spend time showing examples of how to break down, create, and deliver responsive lessons (Chu & Garcia, 2014; Siwatu, 2007). Again, it is not enough to simply tell students that integrating culture is important. That has been going in one ear and out the other as teachers consider all of the actual deliverables they have to produce. They have to be shown how to do it consistently and have the opportunity to practice it in multiple classes and situations.

All teachers need to become educational theorists who, as Gloria Ladson-Billings (2017) explains, "think deeply and seriously about the craft of teaching." Culturally sustaining practice should be reflected in lesson plans, sample lessons, field observations, and program transition points, and it should be consequential for program completion. In addition to cultural competence (including Indigenous language inclusion and revitalization), preservice teachers should be taught how to focus on student learning in terms of intellectual growth sans a focus on standardized tests, which are historically known to be normed on White, middle-class, and monolingual standards.

Teaching students how to think and engage with material meaningfully and critically rather than focusing on what to think would also lead to a focus on igniting sociopolitical competence. This is vital to stretching and expanding thought processes. Students would need to learn to do this dynamically and organically, based on the experiences and interests of the students they have in the classroom rather than via a prescribed static culturally responsive curriculum (Ladson-Billings, 2008, 2014).

As Ladson-Billings explains, there cannot be a CSP guidebook because teachers need to create based on who is in the class at the time. They would need to learn flexibility and comfort with learning and interacting with the culture of their students to use it as the vehicle for connection to content. This would again mean that faculty have to first experience personal growth in this area in order to guide their students through it successfully, leading to changing the face of U.S. education and eventually U.S. infrastructure.

Further Research

More research needs to be conducted on culturally sustaining teacher preparation as an impetus to transform the process and expectations and develop optimal educators prepared to connect with and teach all children from all backgrounds. The current research focused on culture-specific institutions and PWIs is varied with few studies focusing specifically on culture. The context within which teachers are prepared plays a role in the level of comfort in multicultural interactions, as well as the biases they hold and transmit (whether knowingly or unknowingly) about different groups.

If it is not discussed or modeled, or if it is treated as a supplemental add-on to consequential information, teachers will not deem its inclusion as integral to their practice. More research needs to be conducted looking at teacher preparation in general, as well as in different environments (Lewis & Taylor, 2015). This would allow for much needed investigation of culturally responsive teacher outcome expectancy beliefs and whether teachers believe that culture-centered practice will lead to positive classroom and student-specific outcomes (Chu & Garcia, 2014; Siwatu, 2007).

This would also guide the process of changing the curriculum, moving away from a focus on testing to one that centers on the intellectual growth of children. It is easy to include the words *culture* and *diversity* in college and program documents, syllabi, and course descriptions, using terms such as *strives to* and *should*. However, how are programs and accrediting bodies ensuring that the experiences are actually happening at a deep level on a consistent basis? Fasching-Varner and Seriki (2012) call for culture and diversity to be imbedded into every course and professional development to change teacher attitudes toward difference.

This practice needs to be enacted and studied in depth, with an added emphasis on challenging and confronting implicit and explicit biases and limiting beliefs in a space that is nonjudgmental while pushing and guiding students through discomfort. This will allow for the evaluation of true impact on student achievement and school connections. The study presented in the previous chapters adds to information in terms of PWI- versus HBCU-based preparation; however, a deeper dive is needed in terms of how diverse experiences are created and nurtured in urban, rural, and suburban environments for the sake of K–12 students served through both of these spaces.

Preparation is the answer to transformation in American education from the national curriculum to teacher satisfaction to individual student outcomes. Molding practice to include responsive behaviors as indicators of good and appropriate practice as opposed to supplemental considerations will ensure pathways to success for every single matriculating student. Culture and diversity would need to be woven into the fabric of content knowledge, assessment, dispositions, and advocacy while also being a stand-alone programmatic pillar.

Culture, diversity, and inclusion should be their own focused component. This is what would make teacher preparation adequate, propel it into the future, and transform it into a force for change. This is how the game is changed. This is how all teachers become super teachers.

These methods were tested recently in a one-day diversity summit with thirty HBCU and thirty PWI preservice teachers. The group was first asked to rearrange themselves to sit next to students from the other school. They were lovingly pushed out of their comfort zones. The day was scaffolded for them to be able to engage in deep-level culture work and discussion. They were asked to bring a journal with them to privately record their feelings during the sessions.

They were given a tailored memorandum of understanding that delineated what they could expect throughout the day. The memorandum explained that they were going to be made to feel uncomfortable. It was explained that this was transformational work and that they would be better for pushing through the discomfort. They were asked to initial and sign their names stating that they understood what was being asked of them and they agreed to participate fully.

Both faculty and students were asked to be fully present during the experience. No phones or laptops were allowed. Participants were free to write in the journals at any time and were even guided to record their feelings at each juncture when they were introduced to a new experience or conversation. Faculty were asked to model practice for their students in order to develop trust and deeper relationships with students. The facilitator was clear that students would not be asked to do anything she was not willing to do herself, and she too modeled practice and vulnerability.

Most of the work was large group with smaller group breakout work so that the facilitator could monitor progress and emotions. This allowed the facilitator to push and pull when needed, guiding the participants (both faculty and students) step-by-step through the process. The morning sessions focused on getting to know one another, building community, establishing trust, and challenging bias.

There were teachable moments that punctuated the importance of the work that was taking place in the summit. The second half of the day was dedicated to processing these moments, understanding culturally sustaining practice, and students working together to create their own sustaining lessons within mixed groups. Those moments taught everyone patience, understanding, and an ability to listen deeply to the perspectives of others. Students acknowledged misconceptions and defensive feelings. With a little nudging from the facilitator, they owned the process.

The day was difficult. The day was emotionally draining. The day was successful. They day was necessary. Both HBCU and PWI students expressed being thankful for the experience. The faculty also acknowledged the value of the day's work. They discussed being stretched in new, needed, and supportive ways.

One White student stated that this was the first time culture, privilege, and Whiteness were discussed in ways that did not make him feel guilty or personally responsible. He was able to listen, acknowledge, and engage his discomfort. This was the beginning of continued collaborative culture work between the two institutions. They had previous summits but none with this particular focus on transforming how we train and practice.

As Henry Rosovsky said, a greater depth of understanding is indeed achievable if we transform practice. The youth themselves have been calling for teachers and administrators who see them, who care about them, and who are able to incorporate multiple perspectives in their lessons (Howard, 2001). This has never been more important than in the current climate of renewed Ku Klux Klan activity (that is, Charlottesville), people demonstrating comfort in making racist statements (that is, the recent teacher who was fired for running a white nationalist podcast saying she is consciously spouting racist views in the classroom), and racially motivated attacks (that is, police officers shooting people of color out of "fear"). All of this starts in the classroom with whoever is made the center of the conversation and whoever is omitted.

It is time to listen to the children, disrupt the status quo, mitigate marginality, affect change, and meet the needs of *all* students (Griffin, 2002; Hilliard, 1997). As the general focus of transformation has been identified, it is important to note that just as culturally responsive/sustaining practice is dynamic and context specific, so will be preparation for sustaining practice. The future literally depends on changing the game! As this conversation is concluded, ask yourself the following question: Will *you*, as an educator, roll the die and just keep on playing the same broken game that is missing pieces or will you work to create a brand new game that works for everyone?

Ask this question to every single person you encounter in the field of education.

~

Appendices

Faculty Interview Questions

1. What does it mean to be culturally responsive?
2. Explain why you feel cultural responsivity is or is not important to successful classroom outcomes?
3. Describe the diversity of teaching/field experience at your institution (that is, urban/suburban, percent free/reduced lunch, ethnicity, gender).
4. Is culture discussed in a specific class or is it integrated in every class in your teacher preparation program? Please explain how.
5. Have you experienced resistance from students while discussing diversity and/or culture in your classes? Please explain.
6. Discuss your own feelings of resistance in talking about culture and/or diversity.
7. Have you witnessed resistance in faculty members? Please explain.
8. How frequently do you address culture during instruction? Explain.
9. Explain whether you feel diversity is discussed at a shallow or deep level in your teacher preparation program.
10. What are your recommendations to enhance culturally responsive preservice teaching preparation at your institution?

Teacher Qualitative Questions

1. What does it mean to be culturally responsive?
2. Explain why you feel cultural responsivity is or is not important to successful classroom outcomes?
3. Describe your diverse teaching/field experience (that is, urban/suburban, percent free/reduced lunch, ethnicity, gender).
4. Is culture discussed in a specific class or is it integrated in every class in your teacher preparation program? Please explain how.
5. Have you felt unsafe or shut down while discussing diversity and/or culture in your program? Please explain.
6. Discuss your own feelings of resistance in talking about culture and/or diversity.
7. Have you witnessed resistance in either fellow students or faculty members? Please explain.
8. How comfortable do you feel addressing culture during instruction? Explain.
9. Explain whether you feel diversity is discussed at a shallow or deep level in your teacher preparation program.
10. What are your recommendations to enhance culturally responsive preservice teaching preparation at your institution?
11. Assume it is the first day of the school year and in your classroom there are six English language learners who differ in their degree of oral language proficiency in English, their understanding of subject matter content in their home language, and the amount of English spoken in their homes. What are your primary goals as a multicultural educator during this first day and week of school?
12. You have accepted a position at a high-poverty inner-city school with a large population of Latinx and Indigenous American students. What can you do to help all students in the class begin feeling part of the classroom community? What steps will you take to make sure your students have a successful school year and feel that they have a stake in their academic learning and achievement?
13. In addition to his theater performances, thirteen-year-old Robert takes ballet classes three days a week after school. Other boys often ridicule him during class. Would you intervene? How?
14. What are your ideas on ways to enhance parent engagement in the education process?

Program Culture and Diversity Rubric

I. Philosophy and Mission

An important aspect of programmatically infused CRP is the development of a shared definition of culture and diversity that provides meaning and focus for program infusion and transformation. According to NERCHE (Lewis et al. [2016]), how broadly or narrowly this is defined guides and determines financial resources, who participates, as well as the degree to which culture will be infused throughout and become intrinsic to the program.

COMPONENTS	STAGE 1 No Evidence	STAGE 2 Emerging	STAGE 3 Developing	STAGE 4 Transforming
Definitions of Culture and Diversity	There is no program definition for culture and diversity.	The program is beginning to define and operationalize culture and diversity for the program.	There is an operationalized definition for culture and diversity, but there is some variance and inconsistency in the application of the terms.	The program has a formal, universally accepted definition for culture and diversity going beyond shallow application that is used consistently to operationalize many or most aspects of diversity.
Mission Alignment	There is no evidence of culture or diversity in the program's mission.	While culture and diversity complement many aspects of the program's mission, they remain on the periphery. Culture and diversity are rarely included in larger efforts that focus on the core requirements.	Culture and diversity are often mentioned as a primary or important part of the program's mission but are not included in the official mission or strategic plan.	Culture and diversity are part of the primary concern of the program. They are included in the official mission and/or strategic plan.
Accreditation	There is no evidence present.	The program does not include culture and diversity as factors that meaningfully contribute to disciplinary, programmatic, or other accreditation efforts.	The program sometimes includes culture and diversity as factors that meaningfully contribute to disciplinary, programmatic, and other accreditation efforts.	The program always includes culture and diversity as factors that meaningfully contribute to disciplinary, programmatic, and other accreditation efforts.
Historical Context	There is no evidence present.	Culture and diversity and their relationship to the geographic or cultural history of the community are not acknowledged or widely understood.	Culture and diversity and their complex relationship to place are acknowledged but not widely understood, or used to build an inclusive program.	Culture and diversity and their complex relationship to place are fully acknowledged, widely understood, and used to build an inclusive present and future.

II. Faculty Support for and Involvement in Culture and Diversity

An important aspect of culture and diversity infusion within a program is the degree to which the faculty take ownership of culture and diversity as essential to the academic core of the program.

COMPONENTS	STAGE 1 *No Evidence*	STAGE 2 *Emerging*	STAGE 3 *Developing*	STAGE 4 *Transforming*
Faculty Knowledge and Awareness	There is no evidence that faculty have knowledge and awareness of culture and diversity.	Very few members know what culture and diversity are or understand why they are essential aspects of a student's education.	An adequate number of faculty members know what culture and diversity are and understand why it is an essential aspect of a student's education.	A substantial number of faculty members know what culture and diversity are and understand why it is an essential aspect of a student's education.
Faculty Involvement and Support	There is no evidence that faculty are involved in or support culture and diversity activities.	Very few faculty members are instructors, supporters, or advocates of culture and diversity. Few support the strong infusion of culture and diversity into the program or into their own professional work.	While a satisfactory number of faculty members are supportive of culture and diversity, few faculty members are advocates for infusing diversity in the overall mission and/or incorporating it into their own professional work.	A substantial number of faculty members participate as instructors, supporters, and advocates of culture and diversity and support its infusion both into the program's overall mission and the faculty members' individual professional work.
Faculty Development	There is no evidence that faculty are required to participate in culturally based professional developments.	There are few opportunities and dedicated funds to support and sustain faculty capacity for culture and diversity over time. There are few incentives provided (for example, mini-grants, course releases, funds for conferences, etc.) to pursue diversity activities.	There are some opportunities and dedicated funds to support and sustain the faculty capacity to do culture- and diversity-related work over time. There are some incentives provided.	There are many opportunities and dedicated funds to support and sustain the faculty capacity to do diversity-, inclusion-, and equity-related work over time. There are many incentives provided to pursue diversity, inclusion, and equity activities.

III. Teaching, Research, and Service Supporting Culture and Diversity

An important aspect of programmatic infusion of culture is the degree to which faculty are involved in the implementation and advancement of epistemologies, pedagogies, research, scholarship, and service related to culture and diversity.

COMPONENTS	STAGE 1 *No Evidence*	STAGE 2 *Emerging*	STAGE 3 *Developing*	STAGE 4 *Transforming*
Course Infusion	No evidence culture and diversity are infused throughout course offerings.	The program offers a small number of courses focused on diversity. Culture and diversity are infused into course objectives in a few classes.	Culture and diversity are the focus of a number of course offerings. Culture and diversity are infused into course objectives in a number of classes.	All classes in the program discuss and interact with culture on some level. Students are afforded opportunities to experience cultural difference. Instructors offer meaningful engagement with culture.
Knowledge and Awareness in Relation to the Program	No evidence faculty members recognize the impact of culture and diversity in their teaching and learning in the classroom.	Few faculty members recognize how their ways of knowing impact their teaching and learning in the classroom.	Many faculty members recognize multiple ways of knowing, and some incorporate multiple ways of knowing into teaching and learning practice.	Most faculty members incorporate multiple ways of knowing into teaching and learning practices and remain aware of how their beliefs impact learning in the classroom.
Curriculum	No evidence the curriculum is related to culture and diversity.	The curriculum as it is currently constituted is only minimally related to culture and diversity. Efforts to change the curriculum do not explicitly acknowledge the importance of culture and diversity as an asset to innovative curricular practice.	The current curriculum reflects a value for culture and diversity in certain areas and not in others. Curricular change efforts acknowledge the importance of culture and diversity but not consistently.	Evidence of a strong value for culture and diversity is easily apparent throughout the curricular offerings. Curricular change efforts integrate a value for culture and diversity and represent a reciprocal process in which the program changes by learning from new, diverse influences.

(continued)

COMPONENTS	STAGE 1 No Evidence	STAGE 2 Emerging	STAGE 3 Developing	STAGE 4 Transforming
Field Experiences	No evidence culture and diversity are considered in assignment of field experiences.	Field experiences as they are currently constituted only minimally address culture and diversity.	Field experiences are coordinated with respect to culture and diversity experiences. However CRP may not be directly addressed in these placements.	Field experiences are coordinated with respect to culture and diversity experiences. Students receive support in being culturally responsive in the field.
Faculty Teaching and Learning Strategies	No evidence faculty members integrate inclusive teaching and learning approaches.	Few faculty members integrate a variety of inclusive teaching and learning approaches that are designed to respond to the diverse experiences of students in their classes.	Some faculty members integrate a variety of inclusive teaching and learning approaches that are designed to respond to the diverse experiences of students in their classes.	Most faculty members integrate a variety of inclusive teaching and learning approaches that are designed to respond to the diverse experiences of students in their classes.
Student Learning Outcomes	No evidence of the consideration of culture in student learning outcomes.	Few if any faculty have identified the need for culture and diversity learning outcomes for students; student learning outcomes developed do not address culture and diversity.	Some faculty include student learning outcomes focusing on culture and diversity as part of their typical assessment practices.	Most if not all faculty include student learning outcomes focusing on culture and diversity as part of their typical assessment practices.
Research	No evidence of faculty conducting research reflecting culture and diversity.	Few if any faculty conduct research that in form, content, or both reflects a commitment to culture and diversity as an integral asset to disciplinary and institutional integrity.	Some faculty conduct research that in form, content, or both reflects a commitment to culture and diversity as an integral asset to disciplinary and institutional integrity.	Many faculty conduct research that in form, content, or both reflects a commitment to culture and diversity as an integral asset to disciplinary and institutional integrity.

IV. Student Support for and Involvement in Culture and Diversity

A vital aspect of program-level cultural infusion is the degree to which students are provided opportunities to learn about and experience culture and diversity in cocurricular settings. It is also important to measure the extent to which students are aware of, engaged in, and play a leadership role in the development of cultural opportunities in the program and on campus.

COMPONENTS	STAGE 1 No Evidence	STAGE 2 Emerging	STAGE 3 Developing	STAGE 4 Transforming
Student Knowledge and Awareness	There is no evidence of student knowledge and awareness of culture and diversity.	Very few students know what culture and diversity are or understand why knowledge and experience in these areas are essential to their education and their future work.	Some students know what culture and diversity are and understand why knowledge and experience in these areas are essential to their education and their future work.	A substantial number of students know what culture and diversity are. They understand and can articulate why knowledge and experience in these areas are essential to their education and their future work.
Student Success	There is no evidence of student success indicators in relation to culture and diversity.	Few, if any, linkages exist between student knowledge, skills, and dispositions related to culture and diversity and program definitions of student success both within the classroom and outside of it.	Some evidence exists supporting the link between culture and diversity and student success.	Publicly available definitions of student success in curricular and cocurricular experiences always include references to culture and diversity as a critical indicator.
Student Opportunities for Engagement	No evidence of student opportunities for engagement with culture and diversity.	Only a handful of cocurricular opportunities to enhance student learning about culture and diversity issues are available. Very few students are involved or engaged in culture and diversity activities.	There are some opportunities offered to enhance student learning on culture and diversity issues. However, involvement and engagement are limited to affinity groups, and cocurricular programming exists in segregated communities.	There are many opportunities and options offered to enhance student learning about culture and diversity issues in the program and within the larger community. Faculty and staff regularly collaborate with community members to ensure the development of these opportunities.

(continued)

COMPONENTS	STAGE 1 *No Evidence*	STAGE 2 *Emerging*	STAGE 3 *Developing*	STAGE 4 *Transforming*
Student Leadership	No evidence of student leadership opportunities for culture and diversity.	Few, if any, opportunities exist for student leaders to develop expertise on culture and diversity issues. There are few opportunities for students to take on leadership roles in advancing diversity in the program.	There are some opportunities for student leaders to develop expertise on culture and diversity issues. There are some opportunities for students to take on leadership roles in advancing diversity in the program and in their future classrooms.	There are a number of training and development opportunities to develop students' expertise on culture and diversity issues. Students are encouraged to develop inclusive leadership skills and serve as advocates and ambassadors for diversity in the program and their future classrooms.

V. Administrative Leadership and Programmatic Support for Culture and Diversity

In order for culture and diversity or CRP to become programmatically infused, program leadership must demonstrate a commitment to ensure resources, support, and accountability toward that effort.

COMPONENTS	STAGE 1 *No Evidence*	STAGE 2 *Emerging*	STAGE 3 *Developing*	STAGE 4 *Transforming*
Program Policies	Program policies do not recognize culture and diversity.	Program recognizes culture and diversity as essential educational strategies, but no formal policies have been developed.	The program has begun to develop policies recognizing culture and diversity as essential educational strategies.	Program policies recognize culture and diversity as essential educational strategies and formal policies have been both developed and implemented.
Diversity Positions	There is no faculty or staff member whose primary paid responsibility is to advance culture and diversity employed in or working with the program.	There is a faculty or staff member whose primary paid responsibility is to advance culture and diversity employed in or working with the program. However, their collaboration/ work has minimally impacted cultural infusion in the program.	There is a faculty or staff member whose primary paid responsibility is to advance culture and diversity employed in or working with the program. This person is teaching and doing research pertaining to diversity and working with the program toward cultural infusion.	There is a faculty or staff member whose primary paid responsibility is to advance culture and diversity employed in or working with the program. This individual is integral to decision making and functioning within the program.
Professional Development	There is no evidence of required professional development designed to prepare faculty and staff to adequately meet the needs of diverse students.	Professional development designed to prepare faculty and staff to adequately meet the needs of diverse students is sparse.	Some professional development designed to prepare faculty and staff to meet the needs of diverse students is available, but some of it is either inadequate or ineffective.	Faculty and staff have access to an adequate array of effective professional development programs to prepare them to meet the needs of diverse students.
Program-Wide Implementation	There is no evidence of program-wide infusion.	The program is at the beginning stages of infusing culture and diversity as a formal part of their academic program.	The program offers some opportunities to engage in culture- and diversity-related activities (that is, research, study abroad) and courses, but these opportunities and courses may not be a part of the formal academic program and/or are not primarily supported by departmental funds.	Culture and diversity appear to shape course content, project design, and pedagogy. They are infused at multiple levels of the program.

References

Agbaria, A. K. (2011). The social studies education discourse community on globalization: Exploring the agenda of preparing citizens for the global age. *Journal of Studies in International Education*, 15(1), 57–74.

Aldana, A., & Byrd, C. M. (2015). School ethnic-racial socialization: Learning about race and ethnicity among African American students. *Urban Review*, 47, 563–76. doi: 10.1007/s11256-014-0319-0

Ali, S., Rohindra, D., & Coll, R. K. (2008). Student perceptions of a culturally diverse classroom environment. *Research in Science & Technological Education*, 26(2), 149–64.

Allen, B. A., & Boykin, A. W. (1992). African-American children and the educational process: Alleviating cultural discontinuity through prescriptive pedagogy. *School Psychology Review*, 21(4), 586–96.

Altman, D. G. (1991). *Practical statistics for medical research*. London: Chapman and Hall.

Amos, Y. T. (2016). Voices of teacher candidates of color on White race evasion: "I worried about my safety!" *International Journal of Qualitative Studies in Education*, 29(8), 1002–15.

Arao, B., & Clemens, K. (2013). From safe spaces to brave spaces: A new way to frame dialogue around diversity and social justice. In L. Landreman (Ed.), *The art of effective facilitation: Reflections from social justice educators*. (Sterling, VA: Stylus Publishing), 135–50.

Arizona House Bill 2281. (2010). Arizona House of Representatives. Retrieved from http://www.azleg.gov/legtext/49leg/2r/bills/hb2281s.pdf

Au, K., & Jordan, C. (1981). Teaching reading to Hawaiian children: Finding a culturally appropriate solution. In H. Trueba, G. Guthrie, & K. Au (Eds.), *Culture* and the bilingual classroom: Classroom ethnography. (Rowley, MA: Newbury House), 139–52.

Au, K. H., & Kawakami, A. J. (1994). Cultural congruence in instruction. In E. R. Hollins, J. E. King, & W. C. Hayman (Eds.), Teaching diverse populations: Formulating a knowledge base. (Albany: State University of New York Press), 5–23.

Bailey, D. F., & Paisley, P. O. (2004). Developing and nurturing excellence in African American male adolescents. Journal of Counseling and Development, 82(1), 10–17.

Bakari, R. (2003). Preservice teachers' attitudes toward teaching African American students: Contemporary research. Urban Education, 38(6), 640–54.

Ball, A. F. (2012). To know is not enough: Knowledge, power, and the zone of generativity. Educational Researcher, 41(8), 283–93.

Bandura, A. (1977). Self-efficacy: Toward a unifying theory of behavioral change. Psychological Review, 84, 191–215.

Bandura, A. (1986). Social foundations of thought and action: A social cognitive theory. Englewood Cliffs, NJ: Prentice-Hall.

Bandura, A. (1997). Self-efficacy: The exercise of control. New York: W. H. Freeman and Company.

Bass C. K., & Coleman, H. L. K. (1997). Enhancing the cultural identity of early adolescent male African Americans. Professional School Counseling, 1(2), 48–51.

Baxter, P., & Jack, S. (2008). Qualitative case study methodology: Study design and implementation for novice researchers. The Qualitative Report, 13(4), 544–58.

Bennett, C. (2015). Comprehensive multicultural education: Theory and practice. Eighth edition. Boston, MA: Pearson.

Berk, L. E., & Meyer, A. B. (2016). Infants, children, and adolescents. Eighth edition. Boston, MA: Pearson.

Berry, J. W. (2003). Conceptual approaches to acculturation. In Chun, K., Balls-Organista, P., Marin, G. (Eds.), Acculturation: Advances in theory, measurement and applied research (pp. 17–37). Washington, DC: American Psychological Association.

Black Star Educational Institute (2020). Retrieved from http://www.theblackstar.org/about-bsei/

Boekaerts, M. (1998). Do culturally rooted self-construals affect students' conceptualization of control over learning? Educational Psychologist, 33(2/3), 87–108.

Boykin, A. W. (2000). Talent development, cultural deep structure, and school reform: Implications for African immersion initiatives. In D. S. Pollard & C. S. Ajirotutu (Eds.), African centered schooling in theory and practice. (Westport, CT: Greenwood Publishing Group, Inc.), 143–62.

Braun, V., & Clarke, V. (2006). Using thematic analysis in psychology. Qualitative Research in Psychology, 3(2), 77–101.

Bruning, R. H., Schraw, G. J., Norby, M. M., & Ronning, R. R. (2004). Cognitive psychology and instruction. Fourth edition. Englewood Cliffs, NJ: Merrill, Prentice-Hall.

Butler, S. K. (2003). Helping urban African American high school students to excel academically: The roles of school counselors. *High School Journal, 87*(1), 51–57.

Bybee, R. W., & Fuchs, B. (2006). Preparing the 21st century workforce: A new reform in science and technology education. *Journal of Research in Science Teaching, 43*(4), 349–52.

Cabrera, N. L., Milem, J. F., Jaquette, O., & Marx, R. W. (2014). Missing the (student achievement) forest for all the (political) trees: Empiricism and the Mexican American Studies controversy in Tucson. *American Educational Research Journal, 51*(6), 1084–118.

CAEP Accreditation Standards (2015). *Council for the accreditation of educator preparation.* Retrieved from file:///C:/Users/cricha29/Downloads/final-board-amended-20150612.pdf

Cameron, R. (2011). Mixed method research: The five ps framework. *Journal of Business Methods, 9*(2).

Cammarota, J., & Romero, A. F. (2009). A social justice epistemology and pedagogy for Latina/o students: Transforming public education with participatory action research. *New Directions for Youth Development, 123*, 53–35. doi: 10.1002/yd.314

Cartledge, G., & Kourea, L. (2008). Culturally responsive classrooms for culturally diverse students with and at risk for disabilities. *Exceptional Children, 74*(3), 351–71.

Castagno, A. E., & Brayboy, B. M. J. (2008). Culturally responsive schooling for indigenous youth: A review of the literature. *Review of Educational Research, 78*(4), 941–93.

Caszden, C., & Leggett, E. (1976). *Culturally responsive education: A discussion of LAU remedies, II.* Prepared for the U.S. Department of Health, Education, and Welfare. National Institute of Education.

Chamberlin, S. P. (2005). Recognizing and responding to cultural differences in the education of culturally and linguistically diverse learners. *Intervention in School and Clinic, 40*(4), 195–211.

Chavous, T. M., Bernat, D. H., Schmeelk-Cone, K., Caldwell, C. H., Kohn-Wood, L., & Zimmerman, M. A. (2003). Racial identity and academic attainment among African American adolescents. *Child Development, 74*(4), 1076–90.

Chu, S., & Garcia, S. (2014). Culturally responsive teaching efficacy beliefs of in-service special education teachers. *Remedial and Special Education, 35*(4), 218–32.

Cisneros, J., Holloway-Libell, J., Gomez, L. M., Corley, K. M., & Powers, J. M. (2014). The Advanced Placement opportunity gap in Arizona: Access, participation, and success. *AASA Journal of Scholarship & Practice, 11*(2), 20–33.

Cokley, K. (2002). Ethnicity, gender, and academic self-concept: A preliminary examination of academic disidentification and implications for psychologists. *Cultural Diversity and Ethnic Minority Psychology, 8*(4), 378–88.

Cokley, K. (2003). What do we know about the motivation of African American students? Challenging the "anti-intellectual" myth. *Harvard Educational Review, 73*(4), 524–58.

Cokley, K. (2015). *The myth of Black anti-intellectualism: a true psychology of African American students*. Santa Barbara, CA: Praeger Publications.

Colby, S. L., & Ortman, J. M. (2015). Projections of the size and composition of the U.S. population: 2014 to 2016. Retrieved from https://www.census.gov/content /dam/Census/library/publications/2015/demo/p25-1143.pdf

Conley, M. W., & Wise, A. (2011). Comprehension for what? Preparing students for their meaningful future. *Theory into Practice, 50*, 93–99.

Conrad, N. K, Gong, Y., Sipp, L., & Wright, L. (2004). Using text talk as a gateway to culturally responsive teaching. *Early Childhood Education Journal, 31*(3), 187–92.

Crago, M. B., Eriks-Brophy, A., Pesco, D., and McAlpine, L. (1997). Culturally based miscommunication in classroom interaction. *Language, Speech and Hearing Services in Schools, 28*, 245–54.

Creswell, J. W. (2012). *Educational research: Planning, conducting, and evaluating quantitative and qualitative research*. Boston, MA: Pearson.

Creswell, J. W. (2014). *Research design: Qualitative, quantitative, and mixed methods approaches*. Fourth edition. Thousand Oaks, CA: Sage Publications.

Creswell, J. W., & Plano Clark, V. L. (2011). *Designing and conducting mixed-methods research*. Second edition. Thousand Oaks, CA: Sage Publications.

DeAngelis, T. (2010). Closing the gap between practice and research. *Monitor on Psychology, 41*(6), 42.

DeCuir-Gunby, J. (2009). A review of the racial identity development of African American adolescents: The role of education. *Review of Educational Research, 79*(1), 103–24.

Dilworth, M. E. (2012). Historically Black colleges and universities in teacher education reform: Where are we? *The Journal of Negro Education, 81*, 121–35.

Dittmann, M. (2004). Fifty years later: Desegregating urban schools. *Monitor on Psychology, 35*(8), 62–63.

Dixson, A. D., & Fasching-Varner, K. J. (2009). This is how we do it: Helping teachers understand culturally relevant pedagogy in diverse classrooms. In C. Compton-Lilly (Ed.), *Breaking the silence: Recognizing the social and cultural resources students bring to the classroom*. (Newark, DE: International Reading Association), 109–24.

Ducharme, E. R., & Ducharme, Mary K. (1999). Teacher education: Historical overview, international perspective. Retrieved from http://education.stateuniversity .com/pages/2479/Teacher-Education.html

Durden, T. (2007). African centered schooling: Facilitating holistic excellence for Black children. *The Negro Educational Review, 58*(1–2), 23–34.

Durden, T. (2008). Do your homework! Investigating the role of culturally relevant pedagogy in comprehensive school reform models serving diverse student populations. *Urban Review, 40*, 403–19.

Ellerbrock, C. R., Vasquez, A., & Howes, E. V. (2016). Preparing culturally responsive teachers: Effective practices in teacher education. *Action in Teacher Education, 38*(3), 226–39. doi: 10.1080/01626620.2016.1194780

Fasching-Varner, K. J. & Seriki D. (2012). Moving beyond seeing with our eyes wide shut: A response to "there is no culturally responsive teaching spoken here." *Democracy & Education, 20*(1), 1–6.

Feilzer, M. Y. (2010). Doing mixed methods research pragmatically: Implications for the rediscovery of pragmatism as a research paradigm. *Journal of Mixed Methods Research, 4*(1), 6–16. doi 10.1177/1558689809349691

Ferguson, R. (2002). *Addressing racial disparities in high-achieving suburban schools.* North Central Regional Educational Laboratory. Retrieved from http://www.ncrel .org/policy/pubs/html/pivol13/dec2002b.htm

Field, A. (2017). *Discovering statistics using SPSS.* Fifth Edition. Thousand Oaks, CA: Sage Publications.

Fordham, S., & Ogbu, J. U. (1986). Black students' school success: Coping with the "burden of 'acting white.'" *The Urban Review, 18,* 176–206. https://doi. org/10.1007/BF01112192

Freire, P. (1972). *Pedagogy of the oppressed.* New York: Herder and Herder.

Gay, G. (2002). Culturally responsive teaching in special education for ethnically diverse students: Setting the stage. *Qualitative Studies in Education, 15*(6), 613–29.

Gay, G. (2010). *Culturally responsive teaching: Theory, research, & practice.* Second edition. New York: Teachers College Press.

Gilbert, S. E., & Gay, G. (1989). *Improving the success in school of poor African American children.* In B. J. R. Shade (Ed.), Culture, style, and the educative process (pp. 275–83). Springfield, IL: Thompson.

Goldkuhl, G. (2012). Pragmatism vs. interpretivism in qualitative information systems research. *European Journal of Information Systems, 21*(2), 135–46.

Grant, A., & Gillespie, L. (1993). *Joining the circle: A practitioners' guide to responsive education for Native students.* Charleston, WV: ERIC Clearinghouse on Rural Education and Small Schools.

Gregorčič, M. (2009). Cultural capital and innovative pedagogy: A case study among indigenous communities in Mexico and Honduras. *Innovations in Education and Teaching International, 46*(4), 357–66.

Griffin, B. W. (2002). Academic disidentification, race, and high school dropouts. *The High School Journal, 10,* 71–81.

Grills, C. (2002). African-centered psychology: Basic principles. In T. A. Parham (Ed.), *Counseling persons of African descent: Raising the bar of practitioner competence.* (Thousand Oaks, CA: Sage Publications), 10–24.

Guest, G. (2012). *Applied thematic analysis.* Thousand Oaks, CA: Sage Publications.

Gwet, K. L. (2014). *Handbook of interrater reliability: The definitive guide to measuring the extent of agreement among raters.* Fourth edition. Gaithersburg, MD: Advanced Analytics LLC.

Hammond, Z. (2015). *Culturally responsive teaching & the brain: Promoting authentic engagement and rigor among culturally and linguistically diverse students.* Thousand Oaks, CA: Sage Publications.

Hamza, H., & Hahn, L. (2012). Practicing constructivist and culturally responsive methods through differentiated instruction. *International Journal of Humanities and Social Science, 2*(5), 75–82.

Hanley, M. S., & Noblit, G. W. (2009). Cultural responsiveness, racial identity, and academic success: A review of literature. Paper prepared for the Heinz Endowments. Pittsburgh, PA.

Harris-Murri, N., King, K., & Rostenberg, D. (2006). Reducing disproportionate minority representation in special education programs for students with emotional disturbances: Toward a culturally responsive response to intervention model. *Education and Treatment of Children, 29*(4), 779–99.

Hayes, C., & Juarez, B. (2012). There is no culturally responsive teaching spoken here: A critical race perspective. *Democracy & Education, 20*(1), 1–14.

Henfield, M. S., & Washington, A. R. (2012). "I want to do the right thing but what is it?": White teachers' experiences with African American students. *The Journal of Negro Education, 81*(2), 148–61.

Hilliard, A. G. (1967). Cross-cultural teaching. *Journal of Teacher Education, 18*(1), 32–35.

Hilliard, A. G. (1992). Behavioral style, culture, and teaching and learning. *Journal of Negro Education, 61*(3), 370–77.

Hilliard, A. G. (1997). The structure of valid staff development: Revolution, not reform, releasing the power of teaching. *Journal of Staff Development, 18*(2), 13–24.

Hollins, E. R. (1993). Assessing teacher competence for diverse populations. *Theory into Practice, 32*, 93–99.

Howard, T. C. (2001). Telling their side of the story: African-American students' perceptions of culturally relevant teaching. *The Urban Review, 33*(2), 131–49.

Howard, T. C. (2002). Hearing footsteps in the dark: African American students' descriptions of effective teachers. *Journal of Education for Students Placed at Risk, 7*(4), 425–44.

Hsaio, Y. (2015). The culturally responsive teacher preparedness scale: An exploratory study. *Contemporary Issues in Education Research, 8*(4), 241–49.

Hughes, C., Page, A., & Ford, D. Y. (2011). Cultural dynamics in an economically challenged, multiethnic middle school: Student perceptions. *Journal of At-Risk Issues, 16*(1), 9–16.

Hughes, D. (2003). Correlates of African American and Latino parents' messages to children about ethnicity and race: A comparative study of racial socialization. *American Journal of Community Psychology, 31*(1/2), 15–33.

Imhotep Academy (2017). Retrieved from https://imhotepacademyme.wpcomstaging.com/

Irvine, J. J. (1990). *Black students and school failure.* Westport, CT: Greenwood Press.

Irvine, J. J., & Fenwick, L. (2011). Teachers and teaching for the new millennium: The role of HBCUs. *The Journal of Negro Education, 80*(3), 197–208.

Irving, M. A., & Hudley, C. (2005). Cultural mistrust, academic outcome expectations, and outcome values among African American adolescent men. *Urban Education, 40*(5), 476–96.

Irving, M. A., & Hudley, C. (2008). Cultural identification and academic achievement among African American males. *Journal of Advanced Academics, 19*(4), 676–98.

Jensen, L. A. (2003). Coming of age in a multicultural world: Globalization and adolescent cultural identity formation. *Applied Developmental Science, 7*(3), 189–96.

Jordan, C. (1985). Translating culture: From ethnographic information to educational program. *Anthropology and Education Quarterly, 16*(2), 102–23.

Kalyanpur, M., & Harry, B. (1997). A posture of reciprocity: A practical approach to collaboration between professionals and parents of culturally diverse backgrounds. *Journal of Child and Family Studies, 6*(4), 487–509.

Kana'iaupuni, S., Ledward, B., & Jensen, U. (2010). Culture-based education and its relationship to student outcomes. Kamehameha Schools Research & Evaluation Division. Retrieved from http://www.ksbe.edu/_assets/spi/pdfs/CBE_relationship_to_student_outcomes.pdf

Kanno, Y., & Kangas, S. E. N. (2014). "I'm not going to be, like, for the AP": English language learners' limited access to advanced college-preparatory courses in high school. *American Educational Research Journal, 51*, 848–78. doi:10.3102/0002831214544716

Kea, C. D., & Utley, C. A. (1998). To teach me is to know me. *The Journal of Special Education, 32*(1), 44–47.

Kea, C., Campbell-Whatley, G., Richards, H. (2006). *Becoming culturally responsive educators: Rethinking teacher education pedagogy.* Denver, CO: National Center for Culturally Responsive Education Systems (NCCRESt).

Klingner, J. K., Artiles, A. J., Kosleski, E., Harry, B., Zion, S., Tate, W., Duran, G. Z., & Riley, D. (2005). Addressing the disproportionate representation of culturally and linguistically diverse students in special education through culturally responsive educational systems. *Education Policy Analysis Archives, 13*(38), 1–38.

Kohli, S. (2014). Modern-day segregation in public schools. *The Atlantic.* Retrieved from https://www.theatlantic.com/education/archive/2014/11/modern-day-segregation-in-public-schools/382846/

Ladson-Billings, G. (1995a). But that's just good teaching! The case for culturally relevant pedagogy. *Theory into Practice, 34*(3), 159–65.

Ladson-Billings, G. (1995b). Toward a theory of culturally relevant pedagogy. *American Educational Research Journal, 32*(3), 465–91.

Ladson-Billings, G. (2000). Fighting for our lives: Preparing teachers to teach African American students. *Journal of Teacher Education, 51*(3), 206–14.

Ladson-Billings, G. (2006). It's not the culture of poverty, it's the poverty of culture: The problem with teacher education. *Anthropology and Education Quarterly, 37*(2), 104–9.

Ladson-Billings, G. (2008). "Yes, but how do we do it?": Practicing culturally relevant pedagogy. In W. Ayers, G. Ladson-Billings, G. Michie, & P. A. Noguera (Eds.), *City kids, city schools: More reports from the front row* (pp. 162–77). New York: The New Press.

Ladson-Billings, G. (2014). Culturally relevant pedagogy 2.0: a.k.a the remix. *Harvard Educational Review*, 84(1), 74–84.

Ladson-Billings, G. (2017). The (r)evolution will not be standardized: Teacher education, hip hop pedagogy, and culturally relevant pedagogy 2.0. In D. Paris & H. S. Alim (Eds.), *Culturally sustaining pedagogies: Teaching and learning for justice in a changing world*. (New York: Teachers College Press), 141–56.

Ladson-Billings, G., & Henry, A. (1990). Blurring the borders: Voices of African liberatory pedagogy in the United States and Canada. *Journal of Education*, 172(2), 72–88.

Landis, R., & Koch, G. G. (1977). The measurement of observer agreement for categorical data. *Biometrics*, 33(1), 159–74.

Lee, C. D. (2006). "Every good-bye ain't gone": Analyzing the cultural underpinnings of classroom talk. *International Journal of Qualitative Studies in Education*, 19(3), 305–27.

Lee, C. D., Lomotey, K., & Shujaa, M. J. (1990). How shall we sing our sacred song in a strange land? *Journal of Education*, 172(2), 45–61.

Lewis, A., & Taylor, N. (2015). Enacting diversity at a single-gender liberal arts HBCU educator preparation program. *AILACTE Journal*. Retrieved from http://files.eric.ed.gov/fulltext/EJ1092024.pdf

Lewis, W., Wade, M., Diaz, A., Kirmmse, J., Ramos, R., Twyman, E., Millner, M., Saltmarsh, J., Gabbard, G., & Shanks, A. (2016). *NERCHE Self-assessment rubric for the institutionalization of diversity, equity, and inclusion in higher education*. New England Resource Center for Higher Education. https://www.wpi.edu/sites/default/files/Project_Inclusion_NERCHE_Rubric-Self-Assessment-2016.pdf

Li, J. (2002). Learning models in different cultures. *New Directions for Child and Adolescent Development*, 96, 45–63.

Lomotey, K. (1992). Independent Black institutions: African-centered education models. *Journal of Negro Education*, 61(4), 455–62.

Lowenstein, K. L. (2009). The work of multicultural teacher education: Reconceptualizing White teacher candidates as learners. *Review of Educational Research*, 79(1), 163–96.

Markus, H. R., & Kitayama, S. (1998). Culture and the self: Implications for cognition, emotion, and motivation. *Psychological Review*, 98(2), 224–53.

Matthews, J. S., Kizzie, K. T., Rowley, S. J, & Cortina, K. (2010). African Americans and boys: Understanding the literacy gap, tracing academic trajectories, and evaluating the role of learning-related skills. *Journal of Educational Psychology*, 102(3), 757–71.

McCarty, T. L., & Lee, T. S. (2014). Critical culturally sustaining/revitalizing pedagogy and Indigenous education sovereignty. *Harvard Educational Review*, 84(1), 101–24.

McCray, C. R., Grant, C. M., & Beachum, F. D. (2010). Pedagogy of self-development: The role the Black church can have on African American students. *The Journal of Negro Education*, 79(3), 233–48.

McIntyre, T. (1996). Does the way we teach create behavior disorders in culturally different students? *Education & Treatment of Children, 19*(3), 354–70.

Merry, M. S., & New, W. (2008). Constructing an authentic self: The challenges and promise of African-centered pedagogy. *American Journal of Education, 115,* 35–64.

Miller, D. S., & Slocombe, T. E. (2012). Preparing students for the new reality. *College Student Journal, 46*(1), 18–25.

Milner, H. R. (2012). Beyond a test score: Explaining opportunity gaps in educational practice. *Journal of Black Studies, 43*(6), 693–718.

Ministry of Education (2013). *Annual Report.* Retrieved from https://www.education. govt.nz/assets/Documents/Ministry/Publications/Annual-Reports/MOEAnnual Report2013FullWeb.pdf

Mohatt, G., & Erickson, F. (1981). *Cultural differences in teaching styles in an Odawa school: A sociolinguistic approach.* In H. Trueba, G. Guthrie, & K. Au (Eds.), *Culture and the bilingual classroom: Classroom ethnography.* (Rowley, MA: Newbury House), 105–19.

Morris, J. E. (2008). Research, ideology, and the *Brown* decision: Counter-narratives to the historical and contemporary representation of Black schooling. *Teachers College Record, 110*(4), 713–32.

Morse, R., Brooks, E., & Mason, M. (2016). *How U.S. News calculated the 2017 best colleges rankings.* Retrieved from https://www.usnews.com/education/best-colleges /articles/how-us-news-calculated-the-rankings

Moses-Snipes, P. R. (2005). The effect of African culture on African American students' achievement on selected geometry topics in the elementary school mathematics classroom. *The Negro Educational Review, 56*(2), 147–66.

Murrell, P. C. (2002). *African-centered pedagogy: Developing schools of achievement for African American children.* Albany, NY: State University of New York Press.

Nasir, N. S. (2002). Identity, goals, and learning: Mathematics in cultural practice. *Mathematical Thinking and Learning, 4,* 213–47. doi:10.1207 /S15327833MTL04023_6.

National Assessment of Educational Progress. (2019). The nation's report card. Retrieved from http://www.nationsreportcard.gov/mathematics/supportive-files/2019_infographic.pdf

National Center for Educational Statistic. (2016). *The condition of education 2016.* Retrieved from http://nces.ed.gov/pubsearch/pubsinfo.asp?pubid=2016144

Neal, L. I., McCray, A. D., Webb-Johnson, G., & Bridgest, S. T. (2003). The effects of African American movement styles on teachers' perceptions and reactions. *The Journal of Special Education, 37*(1), 49–57.

Nobles, Wade W. "Definition of Power." Retrieved from https://www.drwadenobles .com/#:~:text=Critical%20Concepts-,Dr.,of%20one's%20own%20human%20 beingness.%E2%80%9D

Obrien, R. M. (2007). A caution regarding rules of thumb for variance inflation factors. *Quality & Quantity, 41,* 673–90. doi: 10.1007/s11135-006-9018-6

Onwuegbuzie, A. J., & Collins, K. M. T. (2007). A typology of mixed methods sampling designs in social science research. *The Qualitative Report, 12*(2), 281–316.

Ormrod, J. E. (2014). *Educational psychology: Developing learners, 8th edition*. Boston, MA: Pearson.

Osborne, J. W. (1997). Race and academic disidentification. *Journal of Educational Psychology, 89*(4), 728–35.

Osborne, J. W., Walker, C., & Rausch, J. L. (2002). Identification with academics, academic outcomes, and withdrawal from school in high school students: Is there a racial paradox? Presented at AERA, New Orleans.

Owens, J. (2011). Enlightenment and education in eighteenth century America: A platform for further study in higher education and the colonial shift. *Educational Studies: Journal of the American Educational Studies Association, 47*(6), 527–44 (EJ948990).

Pajares, F. (1996). Self-efficacy beliefs in academic settings. *Review of Educational Research, 66*, 533–78.

Pajares, F., Hartley, J., & Valiante, G. (2001). Response format in writing self-efficacy assessment: Greater discrimination increases prediction. *Measurement and Evaluation in Counseling and Development, 33*(4), 214–21.

Paris, D. (2012). Culturally sustaining pedagogy: A needed change in stance, terminology, and practice. *Educational Researcher, 41*(3), 93–97.

Paris, D., & Alim, H. S. (2014). What are we seeking to sustain through culturally sustaining pedagogy? A loving critique forward. *Harvard Educational Review, 84*(1), 85–100.

Parsons, E. C. (2003). Culturalizing instruction: Creating a more inclusive context for learning for African American students. *The High School Journal, 86*(4), 23–30. doi: 10.2307/40364321

Renner, A., Price, L., Keene, K., & Little, S. (2004). Service learning, multicultural/antiracist education, and the social foundations of education: Weaving a cultural studies pedagogy and praxis in an accelerated teacher education program. *Educational Studies, 35*(2), 137–57. doi: 10.1207/s15326993es3502_3

Rivers, S. W., & Rivers, F. A. (2002). Sankofa Shule spells success for African American children. In H. P. McAdoo (Ed.), *Black children, second edition: Social, educational, and parental environments*. (Thousand Oaks, CA: Sage Publications), 175–89.

Rotter, J. B. (1966). Generalized expectancies for internal versus external control of reinforcement. *Psychological Monographs, 80*, 1–28.

Sefa Dei, G. J. (2008). Schooling as community: Race, schooling, and the education of African youth. *Journal of Black Studies, 38*(3), 346–66.

Serpell, Z., Hayling, C. C., Stevenson, H., & Kern, L. (2009). Cultural considerations in the development of school-based interventions for African American adolescent boys with emotional and behavioral disorders. *The Journal of Negro Education, 78*(3), 321–32.

Simon, M. (2011). Assumptions, limitations and delimitations. In M. Simon (Ed.), *Dissertation and scholarly research: Recipes for success*. Seattle, WA: Dissertation Success, LLC.

Simon, N. S., & Johnson, S. M. (2013). Teacher turnover in high-poverty schools: What we know and can do. *Working paper: Project on the next generation of teachers*. Retrieved from http://isites.harvard.edu/fs/docs/icb.topic1231814.files /Teacher%20Turnover%20in%20High-Poverty%20Schools.pdf

Singh, N. K. (2011). Culturally appropriate education theoretical and practical implications. In J. Reyhner, W. S. Gilbert, & L. Lockard (Eds.), *Honoring our heritage: Culturally appropriate approaches for teaching Indigenous students* (pp. 11–42). Flagstaff, AZ: Northern Arizona University.

Siwatu, K. O. (2006). The development of the culturally responsive teaching competencies: Implications for teacher education. Unpublished manuscript.

Siwatu, K. O. (2007). Preservice teachers' culturally responsive teaching self-efficacy and outcome expectancy beliefs. *Teaching and Teacher Education, 23*, 1086–101.

Siwatu, K. O. (2011). Preservice teachers' sense of preparedness and self-efficacy to teach in America's urban and suburban schools: Does context matter? *Teaching and Teacher Education, 27*, 357–65.

Sleeter, C. (2008). Preparing White teachers for diverse students. Retrieved from http://s3.amazonaws.com/academia.edu.documents/38675437/2008_Preparing _white_teachers.pdf?AWSAccessKeyId=AKIAIWOWYYGZ2Y53UL3A&Expi res=1487265436&Signature=MXPbu%2BXQTsCYI28%2F6%2BvQXqbn2Ko%3 D&response-content-disposition=inline%3B%20filename%3DPreparing_White _teachers_for_diverse_stu.pdf

Smith, D. R., & Ayers, D. F. (2006). Culturally responsive pedagogy and online learning: Implications for the globalized community college. *Community College Journal of Research and Practice, 30*, 401–15.

Smith, E. J., & Harper, S. R. (2015). *Disproportionate impact of K–12 school suspension and expulsion on Black students in southern states*. Center for the Study of Race and Equity in Education. Retrieved from https://www.gse.upenn.edu/equity/sites/gse .upenn.edu.equity/files/publications/Smith_Harper_Report.pdf

St. John, N. H. (1975). *School desegregation outcomes for children*. New York: John Wiley.

Stanley, M. S., & Noblit, G. W. (2009). *Cultural responsiveness, racial identity, and academic success: A review of literature*. Heinz Endowment. Retrieved from http:// www.heinz.org/userfiles/library/culture-report_final.pdf

Steele, C. M. (1997). A threat in the air: How stereotypes shape intellectual identity and performance. *52*(6), 613–29. https://doi.org/10.1037/0003-066X.52.6.613

Teicher, S. (2006). An African-centered success story. *The Christian Science Monitor*. Retrieved from http://www.csmonitor.com/2006/0608/p14s01-legn.htm.

Thompson, S. (2015a). Culturally relevant pedagogy. In *Encyclopedia of diversity and social justice volume A–I*. Lanham, MD: Rowman & Littlefield.

Thompson, S. (2015b). Marginalization. In *Encyclopedia of diversity and social justice volume I–Z*. Lanham, MD: Rowman & Littlefield.

Tomlinson, C. A., & Javius, E. L. (2012). Teach up for excellence. *Educational Leadership, 69*(5), 28–33.

Tucker, C. M., & Herman, K. C. (2002). Using culturally sensitive theories and research to meet the academic needs of low-income African American children. *American Psychologist, 57*(10), 762–73.

UNESCO. (1953). *The use of vernacular languages in education*. Monographs on Fundamental Education VIII. Paris, France: United Nations Educational, Scientific and Cultural Organization. Retrieved from http://unesdoc.unesco.org/images/0000/000028/002897eb.pdf

U.S. Department of Education. (2016). *The state of racial diversity in the educator workforce*. Office of Planning, Evaluation and Policy Development, Policy and Program Studies Service, Washington, DC. Retrieved from https://www2.ed.gov/rschstat/eval/highered/racial-diversity/state-racial-diversity-workforce.pdf

Villegas, A. M., & Lucas, T. (2002). Preparing culturally responsive teachers: Rethinking the curriculum. *Journal of Teacher Education, 53*(1), 20–32.

Villegas, A. M., & Lucas, T. (2007). The culturally responsive teacher. *Educational Leadership*, 28–33.

Vogt, L., Jordan, C., & Tharp, R. (1987). Explaining school failure, producing school success: Two cases. *Anthropology and Education Quarterly, 18*(4), 276–86.

Washington, T. (2012). Lack of technology in urban schools. In I. L. Chen & D. McPheeters (Eds.), *Cases on Educational Technology Integration in Urban Schools*. Hershey, PA: IGI Global.

Williams, D. G., & Evans-Winters, V. (2005). The burden of teaching teachers: Memoirs of race discourse in teacher education. *Urban Review, 37*, 201–219. doi: 10.1007/s11256-005-0009-z

Win, M. T., Behizadeh, N., Duncan, G., Fine, M., & Gadsden, V. (2011). The right to be literate: Literacy, education, and the school-to-prison pipeline. *Review of Research in Education, 35*, 147–73.

Winter, M. (2000). Culture counts: It is the context in which children are raised and taught. *Human Ecology*, 13–16.

Wise, T. (2008). *Speaking treason fluently: Antiracist reflections from an angry White male*. Berkeley, CA: Soft Skull Press.

Worthy, J., Consalvo, A. L., Bogard, T., & Russell, K. W. (2012). Fostering academic and social growth in a primary literacy workshop classroom: "Restorying" students with negative reputations. *The Elementary School Journal, 112*(4), 568–88.

Wu, H. (2011). Constructing culturally relevant pedagogy in Chinese heritage language classrooms: A multiple-case study. *US-China Education Review B 7*, 939–52.

Xu, Y., & Drame, E. (2008). Culturally appropriate context: Unlocking the potential of response to intervention for English language learners. *Early Childhood Education Journal, 35*, 305–11.

Young, I. (2004). Five faces of oppression. In L. Heldke & P. O'Connor (Eds.). *Oppression, privilege, resistance*. Boston, MA: McGraw Hill.

Zhao, Y., Meyers, L., & Meyers, B. (2009). Cross-cultural immersion in China: Preparing pre-service elementary teachers to work with diverse student populations in the United States. *Asia-Pacific Journal of Teacher Education, 37*(3), 295–317.

~

About the Author

Dr. **Chateé Omísadé Richardson** is originally from Long Beach, California. She is an educator, an educational psychologist, and a growth facilitator. She received her bachelor's degree in drama from the University of California, Irvine, her master's degree in counseling psychology from the University of Nebraska–Lincoln, and her doctorate degree in educational psychology from Georgia State University. She has over fifteen years of experience in education and psychology researching how people learn, creating content, training educators, and teaching K–5 (all subjects), grades six through twelve (English, drama, and communications), as well as various courses at the collegiate level.

Dr. Richardson has dedicated her professional work to optimal development, metacognitive teaching and learning practices, developmentally appropriate practices, and diversity and multiculturalism. She has developed and teaches courses on multicultural education (guiding students through the process of challenging biases and limiting beliefs regarding race, class, gender, ability/disability, spirituality/religion, and sexual orientation), African Diaspora and the world (resituating African people in history and acknowledging their historical, global, and enduring contributions), and psychology of the inner-city child (based directly on the work of Dr. Asa G. Hilliard III and dealing with the trauma youth experience in this context).

She desires to merge research with practice engaging in passion projects aimed at optimal child development from conception to adulthood, culture and diversity work for teachers, and transforming the education system from the ground up, beginning with teacher preparation.